How to Be More Decisive

Overcome Choice Anxiety and Lead the Life You Want

D1739095

Calypso Guo

For Dr. Marshall.

Contents

Acknowledgments

Thanks Mary, for your editing chops. Thanks Meng, for telling me people can publish stuff on Amazon. Thanks Dad, for your random bits of brilliant advice. Thanks Mom, for threatening to finish your book before I finish mine. Thanks Alex and Avina, for believing in me and putting up with my endless rewrites. Thanks Allan, for coming into my life and inspiring me to finish.

Introduction

"Decisiveness is a characteristic of high-performing men and women. Almost any decision is better than no decision at all."

- Brian Tracy, prolific self-help author

We all want to make better decisions, the right decisions. But if we think too long and deliberate too hard, we might miss the opportunities all around us. What if you could master the art of decision-making so that whenever it was time to make a decision, you would do it effortlessly? Never again would you waste your valuable time hesitating, worrying and flip-flopping between options and miss the chance to take action. Your decisiveness would create a compound effect: heightening your confidence, inspiring respect from others, and empowering you to tackle future decisions fearlessly. Imagine being able to choose your own destiny.

Many people feel stuck. Perhaps you do too, which is why you picked up a self-help book. Most of us are craving change, but we're not actively inviting it into our lives. Instead of choosing our feelings and experiences every moment of every day, we're passively waiting for society and circumstances to present us with options. No wonder when the "big decisions" (think which career, whom to marry) do come up, we tend to be more anxious than excited.

The art of decisiveness is not taught in schools, yet it is the cornerstone of success and effective leadership. It plants you firmly in the driver's seat of your own life. For most of our lives, we're taught to obey and follow set paths, yet the moment we turn eighteen, we're expected to magically take responsibility and make our own decisions.

No wonder so many of us struggle with this process, not realizing our awesome potential to choose the life we want, one decision at a time. The one mission of this book is to equip you with the tools to **seize the universe's greatest gift to humanity: freedom of choice.** Instead of being overwhelmed by the sea of options and driven to paralysis overthinking their potential outcomes, you will be delighted by your choices and use each decision as a stepping stone towards achieving the life you want.

Benefits of Decisiveness

The aim of this book is to maximize the decisiveness of its dear reader. The focus is not only on making the right decision, but also building a decisive mindset, which will allow you to make *any* decision more quickly and with greater confidence. If used effectively, **this book will help you reap all the benefits of heightened decisiveness:**

Personal effectiveness:
- Increase your confidence
- Make more accurate and satisfying decisions
- Stop missing out on opportunities
- Determine what you really want and achieve your goals faster

Interpersonal skills:
- Gain respect and trust from others
- Become a better leader
- Determine what you want out of relationships

Mental health:
- Take control of your life
- Heighten your focus and clarity
- Stop wasting energy on unmade decisions cluttering up mental space

Growth and development:
- Create a clear sense of your personal purpose
- Design your life according to your preferences and desires

- Break through negative patterns and escape the momentum of the past

"The percentage of mistakes in quick decisions is no greater than in long-drawn-out vacillations, and the effect of decisiveness itself makes things go and creates confidence."

- Anne O'Hare McCormick, Pulitzer Prize-winning correspondent

Who This Book Is For

Perhaps it has crossed your mind that some people are naturally more decisive than others. Perhaps that's true, but it's not because they were born with this characteristic. Rather, they simply happened upon a more beneficial belief system. Far from an immutable quality, decisiveness is a habit reinforced by beliefs.

The good news is: we are one-hundred-percent in control of our beliefs. If you've ever considered yourself an "indecisive person," but still wish to benefit from all the advantages of decisiveness, this book is for you. If you doubt your ability to become decisive, or have even resigned yourself to being indecisive forever, this book is still for you. Because it will **systematically break down the misconceptions of the indecisive mind, and replace them with more beneficial beliefs.**

I wish I had this book when I was younger.

One summer, my employer offered me $800 to entertain his guests from out of town by taking them to the Toronto International Film Festival. Instead of jumping on the opportunity (which came with fun and free movies,) I debated pointlessly with myself about whether I had the social skills to pull off such an endeavor. He asked for my decision later that day, and I said "um." The offer was revoked on the spot.

I always considered myself an indecisive person. I was the person who would mull over whether or not to go to grad school until the application deadline passed. As you can imagine, my hesitancy cost me a lot of great opportunities. More importantly, I had this nagging feeling that my life was not of my own making. I looked towards the future with a sense of dread because I felt like none of it was under my control. The act of making a major decision filled me with so much fear and anxiety that I preferred to postpone it until options disappeared and it was no longer my decision to make.

Leaving my fate in the hands of others and to circumstance was how I got stuck in an abusive relationship for four years. Fortunately, I got some professional help in the form of therapy. It opened my eyes to how I was subconsciously doing things that provoked my partner's anger in hopes that he would break up with me. It wasn't that I didn't know what I wanted (to break up,) I was simply afraid to make the decision. I wanted *him* to make it for me.

The arbitrary path shaped by circumstance rarely aligns with your ideal life path. After years of therapy and independent reading, I learned how to overcome my decision-making anxiety and take control of my life. I am no longer blind to the freedom of choosing my experiences in accordance with my desires. The goal of this book is to share the knowledge and techniques I've picked up over the last few years so **you can get unstuck in the passivity of indecisiveness and use your awesome power of choice to manifest the life you want.**

How to Use This Book

There are countless books on how to do *x* better, whether it's starting a business or texting that person back in just the right way, potentially leading to greater decisiveness in the chosen area.

And while I *could* benefit from upping my emoticon game, *How to Flirt Better over Text* doesn't really help my overall decisiveness. I mean, what if I had to choose between the apple and pumpkin pie at the grocery store but none of the dessert aisle is giving me hints? What then? Isn't it time you had a book that helps you choose between the merlot and the chardonnay as well as between the brunette and the blonde?

I had trouble finding a book that focuses on rewiring old beliefs and habits to increase decisiveness in *every* situation. So I designed this book to work from the inside out:

- **Section I: 4 Illusions of the Indecisive Mind**

  In order to overcome indecisiveness, we have to understand *why* we're indecisive in the first place. This section of the book challenges the commonsensical yet unbeneficial beliefs that plague the indecisive mind. Use it as a mirror to let go of past beliefs.

- **Section II: Foundations of Decisiveness**

  This section is the answer to Section I. It will fill the vacuum of shattered beliefs with new and beneficial ones. Once they sink in, these empowering beliefs will serve as your mental foundation towards greater decisiveness. Use it as a guide to determine what you really want out of life, and developing the confidence to admit it.

- **Section III: The Decisiveness Toolbox**

  This "hands-on" section provides you with techniques and actionable steps you can take today to become more decisive. Each chapter illustrates a different technique, followed by simple, customizable exercises. Use it as a manual to put decisiveness into daily practice.

Inspirational Interlude

Psst.

Yes, you.

You are already decisive!

Yes, you are! **You've been making decisions every moment of every day.** You just weren't aware of it. What did you have for breakfast today? What did you say to your roommate when they inevitably pissed you off? Those were your autonomous decisions, even if it didn't feel like it. At any moment, you have the power to (and are forced to) choose to continue what you're doing, or shift to something else. Wherever you are in life, this moment right now is the glorious culmination of all your past decisions. And your choices now will directly shape your future. That's a lot of power in your hands.

The thing is, we don't notice we're making a decision unless society is holding up a flashing, neon sign. When our high school guidance counsellor asks us which career we've been considering, when our freshly divorced parents tell us to pick sides, when we land that dream job that happens to be on the other side of the country, then we notice. What falls by the wayside are everyday decisions like should I start researching how to form that start-up I've always dreamed of, or continue watching cat videos on YouTube? Should I eat this chocolate bar or a salad? These decisions are just as important and complex as the big ones, and they prove that you have the capacity to make speedy decisions.

We don't notice many of our decisions because our subconscious has dutifully taken the reins. At any time, we can wake up and become fully aware of how much of our lives is made up of our choices. Hint: it's all of it.

Let it sink in that you are already decisive, and you always have been. From here on out, it's just a journey towards greater awareness of all the choices you're currently making.

Section I
4 Illusions of the Indecisive Mind

The indecisive mind is trying to protect itself. Yet it is far more dangerous not to decide, to resign one's destiny to the chaos of chance. The fear of uncertainty and responsibility acts like rust on our mental motors, grinding progress to a halt, yet unable to slow the pace of time. Fortunately, no one can keep being indecisive after seeing the illusory nature of its comforts.

Chapter 1
The Illusion of Postponement

When faced with a difficult decision, it's tempting to say "I'll decide later." After reviewing the relevant information, refusing to commit to one choice is a kind of avoidance. Instead of looking at our options, we're choosing to not look at all. And we've probably all felt the sting of missing a wonderful opportunity because we were busy avoiding its gaze. This chapter will change the way you look at putting off decisions for later.

The Art of Losing Time

Consider this uncomfortable fact: we are constantly losing time.

Instead of viewing postponement as carving out more time to make decisions, we should view it as diminishing the time we have left for anything else, like implementing any decisions we have made.

The past grows as the future shrinks. **What we get in return for our constant expenditure of time is our constant gain of experience.** Like it or not, we're trading time for experience every moment of every day. Our job is to make a profitable trade. We cannot control the price of time, but we have the privilege of choosing the experience we want.

Think about what you're spending time on over the course of a day. You have a finite amount. Are you choosing experiences that bring you happiness and excitement? Are you choosing experiences that are in line with your values and goals? Are you investing your time in skills that will accelerate your life, creating the feeling of saving time? Or are you doing things simply because you did them yesterday, listening to Greg from accounting's inane monologue by the water cooler because it's another Tuesday afternoon? Are you trading your precious time for the experience of anxiously wavering between two options, or working towards a firm decision?

Just by becoming more aware of our choices, we will catch ourselves in undesirable situations chosen by our subconscious. This invites the conscious mind to seize back control and choose in accordance with our higher values and desires. The more conscious we are while choosing experiences, the more practice we get, helping us make better decisions in the future.

The Impossibility of Stillness

Imagine driving along a highway with several exits. A hesitant driver has trouble deciding which exit to take, so he meanders along the path he already happens to be on, missing all the exits. He has made a choice, even though he didn't want to.

Perhaps he's overwhelmed by the speed and complexity of the road, and wants to pull over. But he can only stop himself, not time. Other cars will pass him by as time relentlessly speeds forward. Likewise, what we really want in moments of decision avoidance is to capture stillness. There's something delicious about a moment pregnant with possibilities because we have yet to choose. It feels like we can be on both paths at the same time. But in reality, we're on neither. We're parked at the crossroads, infinitely far away (since the speed is zero) from both destinations. And the more we stall, the less time we will have left to go anywhere.

A self-imposed paralysis is never the answer. Although it feels like you're avoiding risk, doing nothing does not guarantee that your life will stay the same. In fact, if you want your life to stay the same, you're better off consciously choosing the same experiences rather than leaving it up to chance. **Choosing to do nothing does not protect you from the uncertainty of the** future, nor does it relinquish you from responsibility over your own life. It only leaves you more vulnerable to the chaos of the external environment.

We all live with the momentum of the past. The subconscious is a maintenance machine, automatically continuing to do whatever you were doing a moment ago. Changing to a different activity, however, requires conscious effort, just as steering in a new direction requires more care than keeping forward. This is why the most difficult part of any activity is starting it, for you must overcome the inertia of subconscious resistance. It is only through the challenge of conscious decision-making that we can take our rightful place in the driver's seat.

"When you have to make a choice and don't make it, that is in itself a choice."

- William James, philosopher and psychologist

Committing to Today

I get it.

Commitment is scary.

But think of it this way: if you avoid committing to a decision, you're committing to being passive. Consider our interesting use of language: we tend to refer to anything that diverges from an already established path as commitment. We're committing when we're getting into a relationship because we were previously single. We're committing to a healthy-eating regime because we were consuming junk before.

No one ever mentions how they were previously committed to the potato chip regime, or to a life of singlehood (unless they're in a nineties romcom,) and yet their old lifestyles required just as much commitment as the new ones. One could make the argument that the new lifestyle is harder, but what's really hard is the steering. As mentioned before, it takes a lot more effort to change directions than to stay the course. One has to apply conscious intent to overcome subconscious resistance and past momentum. But the new behaviors, too, will eventually become habits maintained by the subconscious. And suddenly you're eating celery sticks like they're chicken fingers.

Believe it or not, **every aspect of your current lifestyle was once something you committed to.** There was a time when having a jumbo-sized TV dinner was a daily choice before it became a routine. So instead of waiting for some arbitrary point in the future to make your dramatic change, observe everything you do today and notice the intent behind your actions. Start by assuming everything you do is already a commitment. Then think about whether you approve of your commitments. Everything from going to work in the morning to the brand of social media you use can be examined with fresh eyes.

Look back on what you did yesterday, what you chose to do. Were your actions in alignment with who you are and what you want out of life? Did you fall into certain actions because you were lulled by the environment and past routine? Do you remember? You might not be aware of every time you're making a decision, but that doesn't exempt you from the consequences.

Instead of giving proper attention to the path we're on or the path we're about to be on, we tend to overemphasize the point of divergence. We dramatically declare our decision to change our behavior, but don't think twice about the reality of maintaining that behavior. This is partly why so many marriages end in divorce. The hopeful couple makes a big hoopla over the act of marrying, the decision to stay together forever. Many overlook the *state* of being married, the daily decision of commitment required after the wedding bells.

All states of being require commitment. We just don't always notice our intent. The patterns in our lives blend into the wallpaper of our existence, so we take them for granted, thinking they've always been there and will always be there. **Only through conscious observation can we awaken ourselves to the immense freedom within our grasp.** Like it or not, we're already deciding each moment. It's up to you to remain conscious of this process, or turn a blind eye.

The Exception

In some situations, you can decide to strategically postpone your decision until a specific future event. The key is that it's a specific future event or potential occurrence for a specific reason.

For example, say you're in a new relationship and are trying to decide whether to discuss exclusivity. Maybe Valentine's is coming up, so you make a conscious decision to decide whether to have "the talk" after V-day, in order to make the decision in light of your partner's behavior on the holiday. In this case, you know a specific point in the future will provide an influx of relevant information.

This is not avoiding a decision, but rather strategically managing information and allocating mental energy. The key is to **make a commitment to yourself to not waste time thinking of the matter until the specific event arrives,** treating the decision like a closed file until the designated time.

Chapter 2
The Illusion of Preparedness

We want to make the best decision every single time. But sometimes the effort to do so sends us into a never-ending black hole of data and deliberation. We often don't feel ready to make a decision, yet standing at the edge can be just as dangerous as taking the plunge. If chapter 1 challenges the avoidance of responsibility, this chapter challenges the fear of failure.

The Mythical Moment

"For a long time it seemed to me that life was about to begin - real life. But there was always some obstacle in the way, something to be gotten through first, some unfinished business, time to still be served, a debt to be paid. Then life would begin. At last it dawned on me that these obstacles were my life."

- Alfred D. Souza, inspirational writer

Many of us are waiting for the perfect moment. The perfect moment to do something, feel something, decide something. We want to wait until the circumstances are just right. The problem is: that moment never comes.

When it comes to decision-making, we want to feel the spark of certainty smack us over the head. We want to have all the information, know all the possible outcomes, and feel a deep inner conviction to boot. Humans are notoriously bad at coping with uncertainty. In a sadistic and hilarious experiment, researchers found that participants experience a lot more stress when they know there's a small chance of getting a painful electric shock, compared to knowing they'll definitely get shocked. Uncertainty equals pain. Why else did Facebook messenger add the "seen 3 hours ago but still no reply" feature? By eradicating uncertainty, Facebook makes us feel good.

But uncertainty is a fact of life. We can never acquire all information and perspectives, especially considering we live in the info overflow of the digital age. (We dumped out more data in the last 2 years than in the entire previous history of our human existence!) Even a relatively trivial decision like what to order at a restaurant comes with a laundry list of considerations: the server's totally unbiased recommendation, the health benefits of each ingredient, and how gluten-free you're feeling today. Not all factors are relevant, but it's easy to get lost down the rabbit hole of info collection.

We also want to feel certain before making a decision, but feelings don't stick. Emotions fluctuate. The feeling of certainty makes a weak foundation and decisions built on top of it will topple over.

Our inability to see the future completes the indecisiveness trifecta. We can make educated guesses, but we can never know for sure. Things don't always turn out as planned. One night, I called my father to cry about the disintegration of my relationship. I asked him to tell me where I went wrong, but he said, "sometimes you do all the right things, but it all falls apart. Sometimes you do all the wrong things, and it all works out." No, my dad isn't Yoda.

Causation is a story we tell ourselves. Perhaps I decided to order the salmon, then got struck by lightning upon leaving the restaurant. The mind makes a connection, but it's impossible to calculate how much an outcome is tied to a decision. Let's try a more plausible scenario: perhaps I ordered the salmon and got food poisoning, leading me to resent my decision. But maybe I would have *still* gotten food poisoning had I ordered the steak, or any other dish at this (apparently shitty) restaurant.

The point is not that we shouldn't try to make good decisions, but that **we need to assess relevant information and make informed decisions while** *accepting* **a degree of**

uncertainty. Only by embracing uncertainty instead of resisting it can we stop wasting time and energy trying to gather all information and control all outcomes. Contrary to the saying, one *can* be too careful.

The Danger of Being Safe

Those who have a fear of flying get jittery as the jet takes off. But did you know that a plane accident is more likely to occur on airport grounds than in the sky? Since they're designed to fly, many fail-safes are put in place for worst case scenarios up in the air. But much less consideration is given to an aircraft in taxiing mode, causing runway confusion and ground collisions.

What feels safe isn't always safe, or the best choice. Although common sense dictates that the ground is the safer option, the plane is actually exposed to more danger when it isn't fulfilling its intended purpose. Likewise, a natural artist might be working against himself if he chooses to be an accountant for the sake of practicality.

We pick the safe, conventional path to avoid danger. But what about the danger of squandering opportunities? Many fear the unknown. But how many fear missing out on something great because they keep choosing everything they already know? Perhaps a plane is meant to fly and a knife to cut, but in existential theory, existence precedes essence, which is a fancy way of saying that unlike tools, we weren't build for a specific purpose. We have the exciting privilege of creating our own meaning.

Since you're thumbing through this book, chances are you already have an inkling of your calling, what you really want out of life, what rips you out of bed in the morning. The phantom keeping people from chasing their dreams is fear. But what are we so afraid of?

"A ship in harbor is safe, but that is not what ships are built for."
- John A. Shedd, author of *Salt from My Attic*

The Boogeyman Named Imagination

One way to mitigate the fear of uncertainty is to take strategic control of our use of imagination. If you use it carelessly, imagination can be a curse rather than a blessing. Imagining multiple outcomes is a great way to prepare for the future. But if you don't manage your imagination, it can spiral out of control.

Consider the decision of whether to move to a different country. Now imagine all the things that could possibly go wrong, from not liking it to getting kidnapped and sold into slavery. The list becomes endless. If you needed to devise a real-world solution for every imaginary problem, you would never leave your room, let alone the country.

When it comes to making a decision, limit your imagination to creating a handful of *likely* outcomes instead of letting it roam free. Otherwise, you'll waste time and mental energy solving imaginary problems, which are tougher than real problems. And this is why:

1. **They are shapeless.** No matter how dire, real obstacles have a consistent shape you can respond to and interact with. In contrast, imaginary obstacles shapeshift whenever they want, laughing in the face of physics. Solve 1 branch and 5 tendrils will sprout in its place.

2. **They are timeless.** Real problems obey the timeline, eventually becoming a thing of the past no matter how well or poorly you handled it. Imaginary problems float above the timeline, where the past can't engulf it and solidify it. Instead of manifesting in the real world, imaginary problems occupy your valuable mental space.

3. **You are too smart.** Many of our real life problems are beaten into submission by our ingenuity. But no matter how brilliant your solution, I guarantee your mind can create an even more brilliant problem.

Exercise 1: Fixed Storyline

One way to use your imagination strategically is to imagine a desired outcome as having taken place in the past. Imagine you have already accomplished your goal, then create a logical sequence of events leading up to your success, taking care not to skip anything that would render the plot incomprehensible to others.

For example, even if it's a crazy goal like winning the lottery, don't just imagine that you suddenly have a million dollars. Visualize actually going to the corner store, picking out the numbers, watching TV for the announcements and so on.

You're challenging your amazing brain to think of one logical path instead of a mess of sprawling "maybes." The beauty of it is that the clarity of the path will inspire you to traverse it with greater conviction, increasing your chances of success.

Exercise 2: Buffering Anxiety

The certainty of the past is an anchor for your goals and a salve for future anxieties. If you're anxious about the presentation you have to do next week, you probably think it's because you're afraid of doing badly. But think of all the presentations you've botched in the past. Sure, they're not great memories, but chances are they don't fill you with fear. The scary thing is not the state of doing badly, but rather not knowing *if* you'll do badly.

As much as I would like to tell you to imagine the best possible outcome, we all know that it can feel deceptive. So imagine the most likely outcome, but imagine that it happened last week. Think about how you went up to the podium, a little nervous so you were quiet at first. Freaking Steve from marketing was staring at his iPad the entire time. You forgot a couple of bullet points in the middle. And then, it was all over, and you feasted on the free bagels.

The past is a relief because you know it happened one way, and it's now buffered by time. The future is also buffered by time, and though it seems like anything can happen, once it comes, it'll only happen one way.

The Distance to Desire

One way to overcome the fear of failure is to think of failure not as an outcome, but as the distance between you and your desires. Few people would be upset if they failed at something they didn't care about. If your mom enlisted you in an embroidery class and your first piece of work looked like the scratches of a drunken cat, it would be no big deal. But failing to get something you want, like that big promotion at work, or that sweet guy or gal, that really stings.

Failure is the state of separation between you and your desires. But if you think about it, you're *already* separated from your desires (as they haven't been obtained yet.) **Instead of seeing failure as something that can happen to you, we need to see it as the default state.** Success, on the other hand, is closing the gap. Success is something that can happen to you.

Trying to get what we want but not being able to get it yet makes the failure state more visible. The sting of this visibility makes us feel like the act of trying pushed us away from our desires. But this is only a feeling, not a fact. Think back to the first time you fell when you were learning to ride the bicycle. As you dusted off your bruised knee, it dawned on you that this was harder than you thought. It felt like you were further than ever from your goal. But that wasn't true. The more practice you got, the closer you were.

"Our deepest fear is not that we are inadequate. Our deepest fear is that we are more powerful beyond measure."
                        -    Marianne Williamson, author and lecturer

When I first read this quote, I thought it was ridiculous. Surely we're not afraid of success. Are we?

The electric shock-happy experiment reveals another tidbit: when given the choice, most participants prefer to control the shocks themselves rather than let a machine shock them at random. We prefer to be in charge of our own pain. Failure is painful, but the pain is manageable when it's under our control. When we refuse to try, we guarantee our own failure, but also find comfort in its certainty. If we dare to try, failure is no longer certain because we might stumble upon success. But people don't want the possibility of avoiding the electric shock - it's harder to face than a guaranteed shock.

Your Inner Compass

Everyone is stuck with a compass to navigate the future when what we really want is a GPS. Imagine how much easier decision-making would be if you could ask about your life path, and Siri would tell you how far it is, how long it'll take, and how bad the obstacles along the way will be. You would thank her, weigh the effort required against the promised reward, and set off on your journey. Or say "nevermind, not worth it" and continue your Netflix marathon.

Technology is not that advanced yet. Our desires act as a compass, pointing us in the right direction. But we don't know what lies in the way. Would the journey be worth it? What if I take a wrong turn into a cul-de-sac and have to backtrack? As long as you're not standing still, fearing imaginary mountains, you're bound to get closer to your destination if you follow your inner compass. Trust in the magnetism of your dreams.

"Once you make a decision, the universe conspires to make it happen."
- Ralph Waldo Emerson, groundbreaking essayist and poet

Chapter 3
The Illusion of Impact

Not all decisions give us an equally hard time. Some decisions seem to promise deeper impact than others. Where you choose to live seems more important than what you choose to do this afternoon. But do the "big decisions" really deserve all our attention? This chapter will illuminate some often overlooked areas of decision-making, revealing a more complete control board of life.

A Fork in the Road

Society places a lot of emphasis on certain decisions, the so-called major decisions. These are the decisions people hype over and awkwardly inquire about on a first date. They're associated with age, and other socially constructed milestones. Keep left on the path of bachelorhood or make a hard right to Marriage Town. Take exit 4 in pursuit of your passions or exit 6 for job security.

The big decisions are a lot like forks in the road. They're visible from a distance, and getting closer forces you to choose. Once you make a decision, you're stuck with it, unless you make a U-turn. Nobody likes U-turns. Thus, the perceived importance and irreversibility of these decisions fills us with anxiety, making it even harder to choose.

But is the road you choose to be on really that important? Think back to a difficult decision you made. Whether it's which major to pick in college or how to tell your partner you cheated on them, it probably felt like your entire future happiness depended on this one decision. But chances are, no matter what you chose, life eventually returned to normal.

"The part of our brain that enables us to think about the future is one of nature's newest inventions, so it isn't surprising that when we try to use this new ability to imagine our futures, we make some rookie errors."

-   Dan Gilbert, psychologist and author

People constantly miscalculate the impact that one change would create in their lives. One study measuring the happiness of a sample size of major lottery winners and paralyzed accident victims as compared to a control group found that surprisingly, there was no significant difference between the three groups, with the winners' average rating at 3.33 out of 5 and the victims' at 3.48. Looks like we really can adapt to anything.

This does not mean that it doesn't matter what we choose, but that **we may be overestimating the impact of one big change.** A separate experiment revealed that by finding something to be grateful for every day, participants were able to increase their happiness, and the effects lasted for more than six months after the study. That's the power of a little change repeated every day.

Tunnel Vision

We're looking for one thing to solve all our problems. It's a very human tendency to project all our inner frustrations onto one external object. Rather than face the complexity of any situation, we prefer to believe in one simple solution.

When I was trying to curb my alcohol consumption, I was spending time on an online forum for people who had quit drinking and were counting the days. Interestingly, I found that while many people were successful in their endeavors (not touching the sauce for x number of days,) they were disappointed by their results. What results were they expecting? Only decreased procrastination, increased sex drive, weight loss, and a happier existence. Sobriety is nice for the liver, but it's not magic.

I was no stranger to putting all my hopes and dreams in one decision basket. My fork in the road moment was when I decided to move to the other side of the world, obviously in search of a total life transformation on par with what the new teetotalers had expected.

I was depressed, and blamed it on the city of Toronto. Having moved there from New York after college, I suddenly lost my friends, lovers, and a community I had known for five years. Instead of rebuilding those aspects of my life, which would take real work, Toronto seemed like a good scapegoat. Sure, it had its flaws, but in focusing solely on my surroundings, I could ignore my own shortcomings.

The decision to move to Beijing infused me with excitement, but the act of moving only lasts a couple of days. I had made no decisions to improve my daily life afterwards. So it stayed the same. I was still lonely, directionless, and a functioning alcoholic. Even worse, I could no longer blame these issues on a single cause. There were myriad little causes, all of which had to be taken care of individually. So I got up earlier, began to exercise again, assigned some projects to myself, and wheedled my way into a friend circle. **A team of small decisions has a gradual effect, but it's the only way to create lasting change.**

Gradual isn't sexy. One big decision that promises to change everything is so appealing that it's actually a sales tactic. It's why you see all those advertisements saying "the one secret to burning belly fat" or "the one trait all successful entrepreneurs share." It captures our attention and fixes our hopes onto one big change, blinding us to more realistic opportunities and perpetuating the cycle of disappointment.

When you develop tunnel vision towards the next fork in the road, you're diverting attention away from the things you have control over along the way, like the state of your car. If the big decisions determines your path, the small decisions shape everything else about the ride, from the comfiness of your seats to the soundtrack of your life.

Packing Our Own Bags

The reason we overestimate the impact of any one event is the disbelief in our own power. We can see the event, but it's hard to see all the things we bring to it - the baggage of our perceptions. We see so much power in the event, the power to give us pleasure or pain, but it's just projection. *We* are the creators of pleasure and pain for ourselves.

Many dissatisfied lovers stumble upon this realization after a breakup. Within the relationship, they unknowingly project all their unhappiness on their partner, believing the other person to somehow have control over their emotions. Then they leave, but the unhappiness follows. Singlehood becomes the new scapegoat. Cue finding a different partner, only to face the same disappointments. Some, however, start to realize they were responsible for their own emotions all along. Responsibility can be a little scary, but accepting it allows us to take conscious control of our emotions. Sure, we can't just will ourselves to be happy. But we can take little steps towards a life that's more conducive to happiness, instead of clinging onto one person, object or experience.

External circumstances are like romantic partners - we chase them to feel good, believing they're the source of our happiness. In reality, perceptions are formed and felt in our own minds. The external world only holds up a mirror to our subconscious. Fortunately, we're entirely in control of our perceptions. We aren't stuck with the baggage our parents and our pasts gave us. We can unpack, then fill it with contents of our own choosing.

Exercise 3: Conscious Creation

For the rest of today, observe your emotional response towards any given event. Anything from buying ice cream to encountering a royally rude pedestrian who bumped into you and didn't even say sorry. Figure out what it is you're feeling towards each event. Write down the feeling, then identify which underlying beliefs led you to this feeling. For example:

> **Feeling:** I am angry at the pedestrian.
>
> **Beliefs:** What an ass. He didn't say sorry because he obviously doesn't think I'm worthy of respect. He probably did it on purpose. The universe is against me.

Whichever beliefs you came up with, they probably felt true. Thinking of the event in any other way might even seem like you're tricking yourself. But this is just a feeling. It only feels weird because your subconscious has chosen the same beliefs for a very long time. So for the sake of variety, ask yourself how a different set of beliefs could create a different emotional response. For example:

> **Beliefs:** The poor guy probably works at one of those places where the supervisor yells at you in front of everyone for no good reason. He didn't say sorry because he's too busy worrying about how he will soon be yelled at.
>
> **Feeling:** Leg still a little sore, but no hard feelings.

We put the personal stamp of interpretation on external events. The more you practice this exercise, the more you'll start to notice how your subconscious often automatically chooses your inner experience. In becoming more aware of your knee-jerk responses, you'll have more opportunities to consciously choose your beliefs and feelings.

Aerial View

One reason people don't achieve their goals is because they don't see them. They're too far away. If you only look forward, you can't see the destination, only the next fork in the road that society presents. And society never presents all the options.

Instead of being overwhelmed by the impending options, we need to zoom out to see the full picture. A faraway destination may not be visible at ground level, but it becomes apparent when viewed from above. In the aerial view, you'll be able to see a clear path leading to your goal (and if there's no clear path, create one.) This allows you to make decisions ahead of time, rather than wait for options to spontaneously pop up. You'll be two steps ahead.

Once you know the precise location of your goal, you'll be able to **create your own opportunities for choice** instead of relying on the wheel of fortune. You'll see the potential each moment offers to choose your values and behaviors in alignment with your goal. You'll see through the conventional map, and pave your own path.

Chapter 4
The Sunk Cost Illusion

A sunk cost is an irretrievable loss. The illusion is the belief that if we just try hard enough, we can retrieve it. This denial amplifies our mistakes, resulting in even greater losses. How can we change our lives if we're making so many decisions based on the past, when the past is what we're trying not to repeat? This chapter will offer different perspectives on the past's relationship to the present, so you can avoid the sunk cost trap.

What Is Sunk Cost?

It's what causes us to make bad decisions.

In one experiment, participants were asked to imagine they had spent $100 on a ski trip, and soon after found a better ski trip for $50. They bought a ticket for this trip too. Then, they found out that the trips overlapped, forcing them to choose to go to one over the other. Most participants chose the more expensive trip, even though the cheaper trip was stated to be more fun, because not using the $100 ticket seemed like a greater loss. But of course, since the tickets were non-refundable, the $150 was a sunk cost, irretrievable no matter how they chose their subsequent experience. So they should simply choose the best experience, which in this case was the less expensive trip.

Irretrievable losses, when tied to a specific purpose, can lead our decision-making process astray. Imagine going to see a movie that costs $10. Upon opening your wallet at the box office, you realize you've lost a $10 bill. Would you still see the movie? Probably. 88% of the participants in this study said they would. Now, imagine you've already paid $10 for a movie ticket, but realize you've lost it upon reaching the entrance. Would you go back and buy another ticket? Suddenly, only 46% of participants said they would. The situation is the same - you've arbitrarily and irrevocably lost $10. But the second scenario feels different, because the loss was attached to a specific purpose.

The experimenters mention that there would be no difference between the responses if all of their participants were androids. An android would place no more emotional weight on the $10 that was destined to become a cinematic experience than a regular old $10 bill. Humans, in contrast, tend to be more emotional in our decision-making than we care to admit.

As explained in chapter 1, we're constantly losing time. Yet we only notice the loss when that time is attached to a specific purpose. We'd be devastated if we lost 500 hours trying to start a crocheting business that never makes it off the ground, (so devastated at this very thought that perhaps we'll decide not to try in the first place,) but we don't think twice about losing 500 hours on Facebook over the next year, silently judging mediocre pictures of mediocre babies, exotic vacations and group brunches. Fortunately, we can use this tendency to our advantage.

The best way to stop wasting time and money is to consciously attach them to specific purposes. We all know $600 is an arbitrary amount until we start thinking of it in terms of 60 lunches. That's 2 months worth of lunches. So the next time you're halfway into the worst movie of all time but just can't tear your eyes away because you've already spent $10, attach the time left of the movie to a specific purpose. Just think, you could use that 45 minutes to finish up that report, prep for dinner, or masturbate. 5 times. The $10 is lost forever, but the 45 minutes can still be saved.

"Decisiveness: perseverance in achieving the goal you approve.
Stubbornness: persistence in achieving a goal you do not approve."

- Ambrose Bierce, notorious writer and satirist

The Past's Echo

We all know that one guy who complains loudly about hating his job - that thing he has been doing for a good chunk of the last century. Chances are, that person is stuck in the past's echo. The purpose of understanding the sunk cost illusion is to free our current behavior from the tyranny of the past. The recent past holds a stickiness created by the mind. It's why what you're most likely to do next is what you were just doing a moment ago, and the best predictor for future behavior is past behavior.

But just because people are likely to be consistent, doesn't mean we have to be. The mind craves consistency. It's a great way to avoid cognitive dissonance. How weird would it be if you closed your eyes and opened them to find that you're suddenly in the Gobi Desert? The mind would try to make sense of the change, telling itself a story by filling the narrative gap with accidentally entering a teleportation device, or getting blackout drunk on the plane. This creates the illusion that the present is inseparable from the past. But consistency isn't a law of the universe. It's a mind-made prison.

One way to escape the past's echo is to consciously choose our beliefs and actions, instead of automatically transporting from the past. Many of our beliefs are out-of-date. When I was studying film in college, I stayed away from anything videography-related because for some reason, I had this belief that I had shaky hands. Then one day, my teammate asked, "how can you draw such beautiful pictures if you have shaky hands?" Maybe I didn't have shaky hands after all. I picked up the camera and was shocked to find that the corners of the frame stayed steady. **Beliefs have an insidious influence over our behavior and performance. Choose them consciously and strategically.**

Another aspect that often falls prey to the consistency trap is personality. Most of us, at some point in our lives, wanted to change an aspect of our personality. But sometimes, it can feel like we're being inauthentic. We worry other people might notice our treacherous inconsistency, and call us out on it. In reality, changing your personality is a lot like getting a raise. People at the office won't find it strange that your financial status suddenly changed, they'll simply react to the current (richer) version of you.

So this is why no one notices when I get a haircut.

You're the only one keeping a congruency spreadsheet of yourself. Others are too busy reacting to the present. And **your present self owes nothing to the past.**

The Neutral Present

The more times in a row a coin lands on heads, the more we want to bet on tails for the next toss. Come on, there's no way it's going to land on heads again. Logically we know that the probability resets for each toss, but thinking of the past makes us all fuzzy. Most people realize it's impossible to change the past, but few people realize it's equally impossible to change the future. The present is all we have to work with.

When the mind delineates the past, present and future as three separate states, it creates a storyline that limits the boundless potential of the present. Contrary to the linearity we perceive, our experience is much more circuitous. We exist in patterns. So when you're telling yourself the story of hoping today to start the hard work tomorrow, you're establishing the pattern of procrastination. When you tell yourself the story of slaving away today to be happy years down the line, you're solidifying the pattern of happiness withholding. And if you're thinking these patterns will magically disappear at some point in the future, well, that in itself is a pattern.

So many of our plans depend on us having full control over our future behavior, but we haven't even mastered our current behavior. **Now is the only time to do and feel everything** you've ever wanted. The attitude and actions you choose to manifest today will form the new patterns of your life.

"The future is no more uncertain than the present."

- Walt Whitman, humanist poet

Blurring the Timeline

Consider the tesseract: a hypothetical 4-dimensional shape that is to the cube what the cube is to the square. It's hard to visualize the fourth dimension, but we can arrive at an analogous understanding by imagining how 2-dimensional creatures might perceive the third dimension. Imagine dropping an apple, and imagine a 2-dimensional consciousness exists on the horizontal plane somewhere between your clumsy hands and the floor. As the apple falls through, the 2-dimensional being would observe its cross-section, appearing to morph from the little bottom to chubby middle to miniscule stem. The apple appears to change, and this change may be perceived as time.

But of course, the structure of the apple isn't really changing, only being perceived sequentially by the dimensionally-challenged. Likewise, what we perceive as change brought on by time could actually be a four-dimensional structure shoving its way through our plane, such that each moment we perceive is its cross-section. Some people understandably see this as a proof of fate, and that our futures are already written. But here's another way to see it:

If the past, present and future are fused, perhaps the current moment is an access point inviting the power of our consciousness to change the entire structure of our existence. Aren't we already doing that? When you're happy, the past takes on a happy tinge, and the future is bright. When you're blue, the past and future seems to shift their hue accordingly. Gives a whole new meaning to seizing the moment.

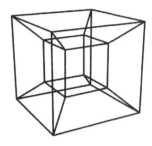

"Using the power of decision gives you the capacity to get past any excuse to change any and every part of your life in an instant."

- Tony Robbins, businessman, author and
philanthropist

Section I Summary

1. There's no such thing as not making a decision.
2. Pretending not to choose doesn't absolve you of responsibility. Worse, it renders you vulnerable to the randomness of chance.
3. By consciously observing our lives, we can see hidden opportunities for choice, revealing a greater degree of freedom.
4. You can never gather all information nor predict the future, so you must accept a degree of uncertainty.
5. We can manage our fear of failure by managing how we use our imagination.
6. The distance between you and your desired state does not increase after failed attempts. They bring you closer to your goal, not further.
7. We often overestimate the impact of big decisions and overlook the cumulative power of little decisions.
8. We aren't completely at the mercy of external events. We can choose our own experiences of them.
9. Zoom out beyond the scope of your next immediate decision to see the full picture and design your own options.
10. When loss is irretrievable, it's illogical to consider past expenditure when making current decisions.
11. The duty of maintaining consistency with the past is an illusion. It slows the pace of change.
12. Break the pattern of deferring everything to the imaginary future and seize the opportunity of now.

Section II
Foundations of Decisiveness

Sometimes it feels like you're stuck with certain character traits. But guess what? You're the engineer of your own identity. Certain base values might be there, put in place by parents and peers, but using the principles of neuroplasticity (the brain's delightful ability to mold to your liking,) you can overwrite ancient cognitive behavioral patterns with new code. Lay in your own mind the cornerstones of decisiveness: clarity in vision and confidence in action.

Chapter 5
Creating Your Identity

"It's essential you create a fiery will from within - harness that power of decisiveness - and choose to be your strongest self."
- Karen Salmansohn, super prolific self-help author

Our identities are fluid, flexible and ever-changing like the volatile cells within us. But after years of experiencing the same belief behavior feedback loops, we've lost sight of the amazing playground of choosing our own identities. This chapter will reacquaint you with the power of conscious identity creation, and invite you to choose decisiveness as one of your many desirable qualities.

Start with Action

While beliefs often dictate behaviors, behaviors in turn shape beliefs. Social scientists have discovered that by adopting a "power posture" (open and expansive body language and an uncoiled spine) participants not only looked more powerful, but felt it too. In multiple experiments, participants increased their feelings of dominance, risk-taking behavior, action orientation, pain tolerance, and even testosterone. Not to mention reduced anxiety and cortisol.

The results of the study are astounding, proving **we can take control of our emotions by managing our behaviors. Your mind will naturally start to adopt beliefs and feelings congruent with your self-imposed actions.** This is because the mind is constantly trying to make sense of the world, and avoid cognitive dissonance - that confusion of when things don't seem to line up. So if you're standing in a confident manner, that must mean you *are* confident. The brain edits itself to keep a consistent worldview.

The more times you think and behave a certain way, the more natural it will become. The brain is made up of neural pathways that light up with every thought, feeling and action. Some pathways are smoother than others, paved with repetition. We have the power to carve out our own neural pathways with consistent behavior, yet how many of us are fully taking advantage of the brain's neuroplasticity?

Consider the self-help trend of finding motivation. The idea is that you'll read something inspiring and motivation would magically fill your pores, fueling you to take action. Conventional wisdom like this is why there are so many procrastinators. The direction of influence is often the other way around. It's action that creates motivation. Many who wait to find their passion in life never find it. Others fan the fire of their interests through sustained action, forging them into passion.

You don't need to wait and hope to feel ready, competent, or that the circumstances are just right before you start. Everything you've ever wanted to feel has been within you, waiting to be released. If you want to feel confident, start by doing things that are often associated with high confidence, even if it starts small at first with a firmer handshake. You might not be able to give a speech in front of an auditorium full of people yet, but you can focus on changes you can make today: maintain eye contact longer, look ahead instead of at the ground, and breathe. Your unruly feelings will come around sooner than you think. You can create your own positive feedback loop.

"The way to develop decisiveness is to start right where you are, with the very next question you face."

- Napoleon Hill, legendary self-help author

Deciding to Be Decisive

With a bit of strategy, you can deliberately create aspects of your own identity. Why not create decisiveness as one of your traits?

Step 1: stop telling yourself you're indecisive. Our beliefs shape our behaviors, and the thought of being indecisive can cause you to waver between options. As an example of this phenomenon, one study found that women who were told the exam they were about to write was far more difficult for women than it was for men did far worse than the other group of women who were told no such thing.

It might be hard to let go of old beliefs, but remember that you may be experiencing confirmation bias - the tendency to only seek out and ingest information that supports existing beliefs. It's one of the reasons liberals stay liberal and conservatives stay conservative. If you believe you're indecisive, your brain is more likely to notice your moments of indecision and overlook moments of decisiveness. We want to be right, even when it hurts us.

In reality, no one is decisive all the time. Show me a person who makes quick decisions in every situation and I'll show you a reckless person. **Chances are, you've been ignoring all the glorious moments in which you *have* been strikingly decisive,** whether it's picking your favorite dessert from the menu or committing to pretending to be sick and staying in bed for the rest of the day.

Compounding the effect of confirmation bias, difficult situations always demand more attention and focus than simple situations. Complex problems are harder to solve. They require more time and mental energy. Soon enough, they're all you see. But what's complex for someone else could be simple for you. So simple you hardly notice. Perhaps you easily and intuitively chose one person between two who were madly in love with you at the same time, but someone else would have lost sleep over it.

As you go about your day, observe each action you take. Recognize that you're choosing each moment. Seize every moment in which you aren't slowed down by drawn-out deliberation as evidence of your decisiveness.

Exercise 4: Following Your Own Example

Think of an area in your life in which you're decisive. It could be at your job, at home, or at the Apple Store choosing customizations. Think about how you were at that moment, and try to transfer those behaviors over to your moments of indecisiveness. If you were authoritative, be authoritative. If you were playful, be playful.

Try to determine your underlying beliefs in your moments of decisiveness and replicate them in other scenarios. Usually, the belief behind decisiveness falls under two categories: "I am an expert," and "the results are unimportant." If you've ever told the waiter to surprise you, chances are you're familiar with the latter.

Everyone is an expert in some field, even if the field is how to defeat the level 37 boss in your favorite video game. Even when I considered myself indecisive, I knew I was decisive when directing short films in university. As the director, I had the belief that only I had the complete vision in my mind, so it was my duty to make decisions to realize this vision. I transferred this belief to other areas of life, believing that I have a vision of my ideal life. It's my duty to make decisions that bring me closer to this vision

Identifying the implicit beliefs that fuel your moments of decisiveness will allow you to spread those beliefs to other areas of your life. For example, a mother who's decisive about lives of her children could have the belief that "I have authority over my children. I know what's best for them," (I am an expert.) She can rephrase this belief to other areas of her life as "I have authority over myself. I know what's best for me." Studying your own brand of decisiveness will make shaping your identity more effective and authentic.

Embracing Transformation

It may feel weird to "abandon" some of the personality traits you've clung to for so long. It may even feel like you're becoming a different person. But just think of the 37 trillion cells in your body going through their own life cycle. Your skin cells completely regenerate every 3 weeks. The cells lining the inside of your stomach turn around in only 5 days.

Consistency from one moment to the next is only a perception created by the conscious mind. In reality, change is the only constant as everything is in flux. Anything can happen in this moment, yet we still cling to the belief that I am already what I am, and any change must unfold incrementally over a stretch of time. By letting go of this unbeneficial belief, we can accelerate our own lives.

The conscious mind has the awesome power to rapidly shift focus, from thinking about what you'll do tomorrow to the eventual heat death of the universe. It can also manifest these violent changes outwardly onto your behaviors. You really can tear yourself away from the third season of that Netflix original and go for a jog. We often don't think of this as a power because it can seem so random. Thoughts arbitrarily assault us throughout the day, but **with conscious effort and practice, we can direct our thoughts to our advantage, and they will ricochet outwards as actions.**

"Those who cannot change their minds cannot change anything."
-   George Bernard Shaw, playwright and author

Chapter 6
Developing Self-Confidence

Few people are born with it, but self-confidence is one of the cornerstones of decisiveness. If you believe you're competent, you're more likely to believe in your judgment in any given situation. On the off chance your desired outcome doesn't occur, you trust yourself to handle the fallout. Unfortunately, low self-confidence feeds on itself. It can seem like there's nothing you can do to improve the situation other than sit in front of the mirror and tell yourself you're amazing, but this chapter will provide some more practical tips to boost self-confidence.

Overcoming Negativity Bias

No one is good at everything. Annoyingly, we tend to focus on the things we're not so good at. We're predisposed to it. From an evolutionary perspective, our brains are hardwired to pay more attention to the problems than the pleasures of life to ensure our survival. That growling sound coming from the back of the cave, potentially alerting us to a saber-toothed tiger, should be higher on the priority list than whatever berries you've been enjoying. The brain also remembers negative events more vividly to learn from them and better prepare for the future.

This phenomenon is known as the negativity bias - what once kept us alive but now keeps us depressed. It's why that one embarrassing incident you had in high school is more memorable than the good days, and why one nasty comment can turn the most gorgeous girl into an insecure puddle.

One benefit of the negativity bias is that it's an alarm bell, alerting us to the substandard areas of our lives, nagging us to make a change. But too much negativity is disheartening rather than motivating. Excessive focus on past events beyond the point of learning hindsight's bitter lesson is futile because there's no going back and applying it. Ruminating over the impossible is detrimental to our self-confidence and present happiness.

The negativity bias is out-of-date in our post-Darwinian society. Everyone survives under the blanket of civilization, not just the fittest. It would be a waste to let ancient instincts reign over your present attitude and behavior.

"Watch your thoughts, for they become actions. Watch your actions, for they become habits. Watch your habits, for they become character. Watch your character, for it becomes destiny."

> -   Unknown, commonly (wrongly) attributed to Thatcher

Exercise 5: Positivity Bias

We can consciously override our predisposition for the negative by cultivating a positivity bias.

Over the course of this week, pay greater attention to the tone of your thoughts. Your inner voice carries more weight than all the external praise and criticism in the world. When you become particularly pleased or scorned by the comments of others, it's only because they happen to echo your own beliefs. Otherwise, what they said would ring untrue, appearing as insincere flattery or jealous trolling.

Whenever a negative thought pops into your head, whether it's about the past, present or future, notice it and balance it with a positive thought. If you remember an instance of failure, remember another of success. If you're focusing on how uncomfortable the classroom chair is, divert your attention to how nice your sweater feels against your skin. If you're anxious thinking about all the ways an event can turn out badly, stop and think of some ways it can turn out spectacularly instead.

This exercise is less about cheesy affirmations, and more about playing devil's advocate. Think of it as a game between your conscious and subconscious. In deliberately challenging the automatic thought patterns that rule your life, you'll view each of your beliefs and attitudes as one of your own choosing.

Celebrating Self-Interest

One of the best ways to increase self-confidence is by looking out for your own best interests. This section is for those of us who are overly nice and automatically defer to others' interests.

Self-esteem is the quiet belief that you're inherently worthy, even if from this moment on you decide to do nothing for the rest of your life. You have inherent value as a living being, and your existence is its own validation. Confidence is believing you're capable of certain tasks, and that you can *become* capable of certain tasks. Self-confidence gives us enough trust in ourselves to decide, and self-esteem makes us aware of our right to decide.

A lot of us are simply used to putting the needs of others above our own, or are even uncomfortable at the thought of being "selfish." I thought my self-esteem was beyond repair, until I read something that changed my belief forever. Imagine your friend borrowing one of your prized possessions. They accidentally break it. Would you feel upset? If you nodded yes, it's a symptom of your self-esteem. Concern over your personal possessions is an extension of concern over yourself.

Someone has to look out for your best interests, and it's best if that person is you. If the thought of fulfilling your own needs makes you feel queasy, you've probably been led to believe that actions are either satanically selfish or sacrificially selfless. In

50

one article, psychology professor John A. Johnson describes additional categories of behavior:

- **Bad selfishness** or win-lose transactions involve seizing your interests at the expense of others' well-being. Examples include theft and emotional manipulation. The bad tends to outweigh the good for both parties, especially in the long run.
- **Neutral selfishness** is comparable to self-care, meditating for a few minutes a day or simply brushing your teeth in the morning. You're doing something to improve your quality of life at no direct cost or gain to others.
- **Good selfishness** or win-win transactions hit the sweet spot. They involve securing your interests in a way that also helps others secure theirs, whether it's trading your $5 for a (very small) basket of organic strawberries or sharing some quality time with a friend.
- **Selfless sacrifice** consists of enriching someone else's (or a group's) interests at the expense of your own gain, though keep in mind a shred of selfishness is always involved, whether it's the opportunity to put that volunteering experience on your resume or the avoidance of social awkwardness by continuing to listen to a friend even when you're bored.

Let go of the binary belief that selflessness is good and selfishness is bad. Practicing neutral and good selfishness allows you to tune into your inner desires, assign value to them, and manifest them in the real world. **As you take action to align your reality to your preferences, you will inevitably create a series of mini-triumphs, boosting your self-confidence.**

Exercise 6: Mini-Triumphs

Start to pay greater attention to those little impulses that reveal your preferences, like cheese or no cheese, and act on it. You can even play with "bad selfishness" when the matter is trivial, like which restaurant to go to. If your friend wants Mexican but you're starving for sushi, make the case for sushi (as long as they're not allergic to raw fish.) Remember, your preferences are just as important as anyone else's, and it's high time you validated them.

If you're having trouble getting started, downsize. Select your preference on the smallest possible scale. If some people in the office want the window open and some want it closed, and you want it closed, close it. Over time, you will be able to scale up, creating a habit of picking your preference and creating it in your reality, which will improve your confidence and decisiveness.

Confronting Fear

Jia Jiang is an entrepreneur who was deeply afraid of rejection. His fear kept him from making proposals to potential investors, crippling his chances for success. Instead of running away from his fear, Jia faced it head on by devising the 100 Days of Rejection challenge. Throughout this process, which he called rejection therapy, he made one outrageous request per day, like asking to borrow $100 from a total stranger. The requests were designed to elicit a no, the idea being that continued exposure to rejection would desensitize him to it.

It worked. Fear shrinks when we face it and amplifies if we turn away. Jia overcame his fear of rejection not only through desensitization, but also by learning more about his fear along the way. One day, he knocked on the door of a random house and asked the homeowner if he could plant a flower in his backyard.

The homeowner rejected him, but then explained that it was because he had a dog that loves to dig up foliage. Jia was pleasantly shocked that the rejection had nothing to do with the homeowner not trusting him, or finding him weird, and everything to do with his cuddly companion.

As you face your fears, they inevitably become more familiar, and the familiar is seldom scarier than the unknown. Plus, Jia got some surprise yesses along the way too, including the Dunkin Donuts employee who heroically accepted his request to make Olympic symbol donuts (5 multicolored, interlinking donuts in Olympic fashion.) Hey, you never know.

We confront fear by greeting the thing it clings to, and we've been doing this since we were kids. Throughout our childhood, we were forced to confront our fears, whether they were strange faces the folds of our blanket made at night, learning to ride a bike, or the first day of school. **Feeling the knot in our stomach and doing it anyway was a crucial part of growing up, and still is.** It reassures us that we have the power to overcome adversity and handle the challenges life throws in our way.

Now that we've become adults, our fears have also become more complex, transforming from monsters under the bed to more psychological demons. But the process of taming them remains the same. Soon enough, what seemed like the impossible feat of getting along with so many strangers becomes just another day of middle school. If you face the nagging fears that are keeping you back in life, you will grow as a person and improve your confidence immeasurably.

Exercise 7: Facing Fears

Start with something small that bothers you frequently. If you have social anxiety, and have trouble communicating with others, aim to ask one question to someone every day, anything from their philosophical outlook on life to what time is it. If that's too tough, start by just being in the presence of someone, even a stranger.

For example, I was always afraid of cutting ties with people, even if their only contribution to my life was negative. They might dislike me for it, or turn out to be secretly brilliant underneath. I started off by simply taking a deep breath and not responding to their message, at least not tonight, not this time. Eventually, I graduated to more mature strategies of ceasing communication. Every step you take towards your fears brings you one step closer to eradicating them.

Recognizing Resilience

It was hard deciding whether to break up with my boyfriend. I wavered for years over this decision. As you can imagine, it caused palpable pain for both parties. Then, my therapist asked me something interesting. What's the worst case scenario? I was afraid of irrevocable loss, and my greatest fear was that he would never speak to me again. He asked if that were to happen, would I be able to cope? It was a rhetorical question. And I said yes.

It dawned on me that humans have the ability to cope with myriad adverse scenarios. One stunning proof of human resilience revealed itself in the 1972 Andes plane crash. Survivors persisted for a record 72 days, feeding on the remains of dead passengers before a rescue team finally showed up. Yup. As a more down-to-earth example, ask someone what they would do if they lost their job and you'd hear their mind shifting gears.

The brain is designed to solve problems, and it does this with the utmost efficiency when problems arise. It's so efficient that it has time to work on imaginary problems, trying to see every possible outcome of every decision, then attempting the impossible puzzle of choosing the best option. The thing that scares us most is not the worst outcome, but rather thinking we're responsible for the worst outcome, and could have somehow avoided it. The freedom to influence your future is scary, but it becomes a little less scary when you remember that you have the resilience to handle any outcome.

Chapter 7
Overcoming Anxiety About the Future

One of the greatest impediments to decisiveness is the attachment to a particular vision of the future. You'll try to do everything "right" in order to achieve that image, while knowing deep down it's impossible to have full control over how the future unfolds. This chapter will help you let go of the ideal outcome so you can overcome overanalysis paralysis.

Detaching from Outcome

Attachment is the overarching need for a person, object, or state to feel complete. If you're attached to a romantic partner, for example, being with them starts to seem more like a need than a preference. It can lead to compromising your core values just to preserve the relationship, because your sense of identity depends on it. A parallel is seen in the workaholic who compromises their health and family. Chances are, their sense of identity is tied to their work performance.

Many of us are attached to the outcome of our decisions. The symptoms are not as severe as the attachment to a person, but the effects are profound. If you're making decisions based solely on what you predict will be the outcome, like choosing an administrative job to afford a financially stable future when what you really want is to be a musician, you're missing out on the magic of choosing your desires.

Choosing between what seems to promise a desirable outcome and what's desirable now creates a psychological rift. This rift feels like indecision. Even if you choose one, you will pine for the other, question if you made the right decision, and continually think about dropping everything for the other option. There's always a tension between the present and the future. It's why we procrastinate.

To solidify a decision, you must bridge the rift by shifting your perspective. If you choose administration for future security, you have to create an element of desire in the present. Think of everything you *already* enjoy about the career. Think of the benefits of the outcome not as potential future rewards, but desirable qualities intrinsic to the job. If you choose to be a rockstar, trust in the power of your desire to shape the odds.

Choosing in accordance with desires and higher values manifests them in reality while choosing based on predicted outcomes cements old patterns. The flaw of prediction lies in the fact that we can never be sure, and the prediction itself often creates a self-fulfilling prophesy. Our predictions are based on the results of other people and our own results in the past. You might predict failure as a salesperson because you tried but didn't make any sales in the first 2 months. If you believe this prediction, you'll definitely make it happen by quitting. Choosing based on past patterns is sure to replicate them in the future. But if you really want to be a salesperson and are committed to putting in the work, you'll sharpen your skills and create an unexpected future.

Funny story: it took me years to learn to ride the bicycle. I'd like to think it wasn't because I had horrible motor control skills, but because I had started in my adult years. As an adult with an over-analytical mind, each scrape of the knee became a scrape of the ego. Each fall made me predict that I would never be able to learn. I quit many times. Children don't have this tendency. No matter how many times they fall, they don't bother predicting whether they'll learn to walk. Their desire to run drives them to stand up again.

If you believe in the awesome malleability of the future, your desired state will draw you towards it like a magnet.

"You can't connect the dots looking forward; you can only connect them looking backwards. So you have to trust that the dots will somehow connect in your future."

- Steve Jobs, visionary entrepreneur and inventor

Shaping Your Reality

Ever had the experience of getting out of bed on a high note, and had your happiness amplified by chance events throughout the day? Or being in a humdrum mood and having your external environment exacerbate it, like non-peripheral-vision-having people bumping against you on the sidewalk? It's less a mystical force in the universe and more another example of confirmation bias. Since you feel happy, the world must be full of happy things, so you subconsciously select to perceive only positive cues from the environment.

We're constantly shaping our current reality with our thoughts, which radiate outward as actions, and in turn, affect future outcomes. Think of your current state as an outcome of the past, and try to determine which key decisions led you to this outcome. There are the big ones, like working in the field you chose as your major, and living in the city you chose to move to. But when you look at your minor dissatisfactions in life, like being a few pounds over your ideal weight or not having as many friends as you'd like, chances are it's hard to tie them to a specific decision you made in the past.

"What we anticipate seldom occurs; what we least expected generally happens."

- Benjamin Disraeli, former Prime Minister of the UK and novelist

Part of why the future is so hard to predict is because it doesn't depend solely on one decision, or even two. Rather, **each moment is a decision that contributes to the outcome.** The future is complex, just like the present. How can we manage every aspect of the future when we can't even manage every aspect of the present? No one can reach the perfect outcome because no one can take conscious control of each moment. But you can come close. By becoming aware of more subtle opportunities for choice, you gain a greater degree of influence over your future.

Projecting Your Desired State

We're bombarded by options every day. Think of how many brands of breakfast cereal there are to choose from. Instead of attaching each option to a predicted outcome, create a vision of your ideal outcome. Amidst the shifting kaleidoscope of options, this vision will act as your anchored focus, so you can make each decision in alignment with your desired state.

Instead of overemphasizing the weight of each decision you have to make, see each moment as an opportunity to get closer to your ideal state. For example, say an ambitious 17-year-old's vision involves wealth and social status, and he's having a hard time deciding between studying law and finance. If he has the aptitude for both, then *both* options will bring him closer to his vision. Stalling on the decision, however, will not bring him closer to his vision, as it's a waste of time. During that time, he could be investing in other activities that will bring him closer to his ideal state, like studying after class, researching internship and job opportunities, getting adequate sleep and so on.

Many important choices in life do not present themselves as decisions. Your guidance counsellor will ask which major you're considering, but no one will ask you every night whether you will study or play video games. Chances are, you won't either, except in the brief moment of panic upon realizing that you've been raiding villages for the past 4 hours. Our daily behavior is dictated by what we feel like doing, and our habits, squandering the subtle opportunities for conscious choice. And it's these choices that ultimately affect the kid's chances of future success, much more than the one-time decision of law versus finance.

Cultivating a strong vision of your ideal state is like finding the destination of your life's path. You might not know how you'll get there, but keeping your eyes on the destination naturally steers you in the right direction, and you can recalibrate after a wrong turn. No longer will you drift aimlessly, distracted by irrelevant options. For example, a career change is possible in most people's lives, and each new career promises its own colorful outcome. But if your current career already matches with your ideal or is bringing you closer to it, there's no need to waste energy looking at the what ifs. Instead, focus that attention on misalignments in other areas of your life. For example, if your ideal state includes being in shape but you're overweight, focus on making dietary and fitness decisions that will bring you closer to your goal.

The world is not in control of your options. *You* are in control of your options. Society and situations simply have a way of framing and highlighting them. Look through the limiting social construct of life's major decisions, and you will see that the degree of freedom you have is delightfully overwhelming. In order to avoid getting lost in the vast number of possibilities, trust in your ability to steer yourself towards your desired outcome.

Chapter 8
What Do You Really Want?

It's important to know what you want. The mere existence of goals increases your chances of getting there. But knowing what you want is half the battle for the indecisive person. With so much freedom and opportunity in the world, it can be hard to commit to one option. This chapter will help you achieve a deeper understanding of desire so you can discover what you really want.

4 Types of Desire

Most of us have been confused by our desires. Sometimes you want something, but you're not sure you want it, but it's not good for you, but it completely goes against something else you want, but your friends make fun of you. Many desires seem contradictory, but a closer look often reconciles them. A description of the 4 different types of desire are as follows:

1. **Idealistic Desires:** If someone asks you what you want out of life, you'll answer with your idealistic desires. I want to be rich. I want to be famous. I want to leave a legacy. These desires are identity-focused. You do want the actual money, but what you really want is the state of being rich, and all that it implies, that you were brilliant and persistent enough to get there. Idealistic desires spark ambition, but also a sense of lack. It creates a sometimes painful rift between your ideal state and your current reality

2. **Outlet Desires:** Everything you truly enjoy doing is an outlet desire. Hanging out with friends, dancing, reading, traveling. Outlet desires are activity-focused, and these activities are an outlet for your social, artistic and other impulses. It's possible to achieve a state of flow (a period of uninterrupted focus and joy while engaging in a

challenging and fulfilling activity) while pursuing your outlet desires.

3. **Distractive Desires:** Distractive desires are focused on easy to attain but low-quality pleasures, like surfing social media, eating cheese puffs, and recreational drugs. Unlike outlet desires, distractive desires don't arise from an inner impulse, but rather distracting stimuli in the external environment. Despite the inevitable dissatisfaction of pursuing low-quality pleasures, the activities that distractive desires lead you to are addictive because almost no effort is required. The reward to effort ratio is high, but the reward itself isn't worth trading your valuable time for.

4. **Fixative Desires:** Fixation is the excessive preoccupation with a person, place or thing. Fixative desires are the unreasonable and often obsessive need for anything from the latest iPhone to your married coworker. If satisfied, they offer temporary pleasure. If out of reach, they inflict intense psychological pain. Fixative desires arise from the subconscious belief that you're incomplete, which creates the illusion that the desired object holds vital importance, and obtaining it will make you complete.

If these desires are pulling you in opposing directions, they create inertia. To streamline your path towards your desired state, it's crucial to reconcile the conflict between these desires.

Reconciling Desires

We all wish to achieve our idealistic desires, but our distractive desires often pull us in the opposite direction. Perhaps you want to be fit, but you really want to eat this bag of chips. Perhaps you want to enrich your mind with wisdom, but you really want to watch these two trolls battle it out in the internet comment thread arena. Perhaps you want to be sober, but you really want this beer.

The solution lies not in willpower. Banning distractions simply doesn't work in the long run. Idealistic desires create stress, and distractive desires temporarily alleviate it. This is because idealistic desires highlight the separation between your current self and your ideal self, and challenges you to bridge the daunting gap. If you wish to be a great writer, you should practice writing. But sometimes the magnitude of your idealistic desires is so intimidating that just the thought of writing a couple of words can trigger an anxiety attack.

Outlet desires have the same soothing effect as distractive desires with none of the guilt, but we often choose distractive desires in moments of stress because they're easier to obtain. If you're already stressed about writing your first masterpiece, organizing an impromptu get-together with friends seems like added stress, but social media is only a click away. Instant gratification. Over time, choosing distractive desires over outlet desires becomes a habit, causing us to ignore outlet desires even when they're readily available.

To obtain our idealistic desires, we must undertake a collection of activities, some of them unpleasant. For example, to become an ivy league student, you should study, pay attention in class, join extracurricular activities and so on. If most of these obligatory activities coincide with your outlet desires, there would be much less tension, and this tension is what causes stress and the compulsion towards distractive desires. **In the best case scenario, the day-to-day components of your idealistic desires mostly coincide with the activities in your outlet desires,** but this is not the case for many people. If your idealistic desires frequently cause friction in your life, it's time to examine them further.

Deconstructing Desires

Idealistic desires are created as the ego finds its place in society. Unlike outlet desires, which arise from an inner impulse, idealistic desires are learned, and can be unlearned. Sometimes, you form your idealistic desires based on your outlet desires, and sometimes they're imposed upon you by parents or society, or most insidiously, by yourself.

Maybe you watched a movie when you were little and fell in love with the idea of being a leader, say a CEO. But you're uncomfortable having authority over others, as you're more egalitarian by nature. In this scenario, the idealistic desire of becoming a CEO would be stress-inducing, and even achieving wouldn't relieve the stress, because you like the idea of being the boss rather than the reality of its day-to-day components.

They're called idealistic desires because they're based on ideals rather than practical considerations. If your idealistic desires are completely at odds with your outlet desires, like if you're an aspiring painter who hates the act of painting, it's time to figure out why you want it in the first place.

When analyzing the source of your idealistic desires, it's important to stay open-minded. Even desires you've had since you were little shouldn't be exempt from scrutiny. It's entirely possible that when you were 4-years-old, someone you looked up to casually remarked that being a doctor is the most honorable profession in the world, and ever since then, you've wanted to be a doctor, even though the thought of blood makes you faint. If we stay stubbornly loyal to our desires, we might build our entire futures on the romanticism of a chance event.

Another technique is to ask yourself what fringe benefits you stand to gain if you accomplish your idealistic desires. For example, if you do become a doctor, you'd gain social status, a high salary, the pride of saving lives, and a cool lab coat. And if the day-to-day components of being a doctor are mostly at odds with your outlet desires, you can ask yourself which other careers offer you the same things, minus the lab coat.

You should also keep questioning what you want until you arrive at something fundamental. If you want social status, ask yourself why. If you want a high salary, ask yourself why. If you answered to buy cool gadgets, ask yourself why you want them. Chances are, your desires boil down to a desire for a feeling, like wanting to feel loved, or wanting to feel powerful. To combat fixative desires, recognize that you have the power to create these feelings within yourself. You don't have to wait until you've accomplished something to feel a certain way.

Exercise 8: Identifying Unbeneficial Beliefs

Sometimes, your outlet desires, which should bring pleasure, create anxiety instead. This occurs when they overlap with your idealistic desires. You could genuinely love writing, but the activity started filling you with dread the day you decided to become a world-famous author. Idealistic desires often attach implicit beliefs and obligations to an otherwise innocent activity. In this case, the subconscious beliefs might be:

- Every word I write must be a masterpiece. (I need my behavior to be congruent with my idealized identity at all times.)
- If I don't write well in this sitting, I'll never accomplish my goal because I'm untalented.
- I might never live up to my ideal self.

Oftentimes, all it takes to quash unbeneficial beliefs is to become cognizant of them. Once you determine the beliefs that are sabotaging your progress, consciously observe your thoughts and catch them as they come to replace them with beneficial beliefs like:

- No one creates masterpieces on their first try.

- Practice is guaranteed to make me better.
- The time I devote to this task can only bring me closer to my goal.

If the pressure embedded in your idealistic desire is impeding you from achieving it, reframe it as an activity-based goal instead of an identity-based goal. Replace the pass or fail goal of "I'll be a successful writer one day" with the ongoing and easily achievable goal of "I'll write for an hour every day." The lack of expectations for the uncertain future will increase your focus on the task at hand, and minimize stress, making you less likely to succumb to distractive desires.

Cultivating Desires

If you happen to not have any idealistic desires, you're not in a bad place. You've escaped from organically forming your goals based on random encounters with societal ideals, and are free to **strategically cultivate your desires in alignment with your values and aptitudes. You have the pleasure of building the pyramid from the bottom-up instead of the top-down.** First, imagine what you want each day to look like. Then, determine which life path naturally includes those days. Not knowing what you want yet is a gift, for you're free from preconceived notions of what you should want.

Breaking Destructive Patterns

Most of us have had the experience of inexplicably choosing something we say we don't want over and over again. The classic example is the person who wants a relationship with someone who treats them with respect, but repeatedly ends up with jerks. Oftentimes it's not that they're a bad judge of character. They intuitively know their new prospect will treat them badly, but they choose them anyway.

The conscious and educated mind knows what's good for it, but is often undermined by the subconscious. Unlike the rational mind, the subconscious mind clings to the familiar because it fears the unknown. In the case of subpar partners, the subconscious is not only replicating past relationship patterns, but also the relationship dynamics between you and your primary caregivers. After all, we learn about love from our parents. When the conscious mind gets burned out through overuse, the subconscious mind takes over and chooses what you're used to, keeping you mired in old patterns.

Breaking destructive patterns requires not force, but understanding. **Instead of stubbornly resisting old tendencies (which often makes them seem more tempting), ask yourself what you *enjoy* about the pattern.** Even misery contains pleasure. For example, I liked to write very unconventional screenplays (think David Lynch, and those "no one knows what's going on" movies). Eventually, I wanted to write a mainstream script. But every time I tried, I ended up with another unconventional script. It took me a while to realize that the "enjoyment" I got out of this pattern was from being able to deflect every bit of criticism I got with "you're not supposed to get it anyway." Upon realizing this, I finally wrote something that made sense to someone other than myself.

Finding the shred of desire hidden in destructive patterns is like finding the missing puzzle piece. If you knows the whys of your behavior, it becomes easier to control. If you suspect you're used to failing, and are subconsciously sabotaging your own success, monitor your feelings to determine what you like about the pattern. Maybe it feels good to be comforted by friends and family after a failure. Remove the comfort. Stop sharing your downfalls with others. Maybe you feel relieved that others won't be intimidated by your success. Change your belief. Recognize that you aren't responsible for other people's feelings; they are. Determine what you like about the patterns you hate, and eradicate them.

Become aware of beliefs that sabotage your desires. Oftentimes, harmful beliefs are subtle enough to go unnoticed. If you ask someone whether they think they're attractive, they might say yes, but still have the thought "I am unattractive" multiple times a day. Your beliefs are not always what you think they are, rather they're revealed in the frequency of your thoughts. If you choose your thoughts and beliefs consciously and strategically, you can achieve your desires with minimal psychological resistance.

Section II Summary

1. You have the freedom to radically change your identity. Thanks to the mind's need for consistency, you can evoke feelings and beliefs within yourself by simply adopting the corresponding behaviors. By focusing your attention on the instances in which you *have* been decisive, you can create a belief behavior feedback loop.

2. The best way to develop self-confidence is to practice aligning your reality to your preferences. Get comfortable listening to your own interests, and choose them frequently. Minimize your fears by taking small steps towards exposing yourself to them. Humans are incredibly resilient creatures that can usually handle any outcome. It's uncertainty that scares us.

3. We're all afraid of making the wrong decision, but the reality is that no one decision is attached to a particular outcome. Instead, our outcomes are a culmination of all our past decisions, even the ones we don't remember making. Thus, instead of trying to predict the future, we should become more aware of our thoughts so we can make choices that create the future we desire.

4. Know what you truly want. Desires often seem to contradict each other, and only by aligning them can you achieve your goals smoothly. It's important to find joy in the activities that bring you closer to your goal, lest you become overwhelmed with stress and turn to distractions. To break negative patterns in your life, pinpoint the hidden pleasure within the pattern.

Section III
The Decisiveness Toolbox

Decisiveness is a skill, and skills take practice to develop and perfect. Now that you've established the mindset of decisiveness, it's time to proceed to action. This section will present a series of mental techniques, visualization exercises, helpful habits and practical steps to kickstart your journey towards mastering decisiveness.

Chapter 9
The Art of Meditation

The varied and spectacular benefits of meditation are well-known. But did you know it can even help you become more decisive? The practice of meditation paves the path towards mastering any skill because it increases the awareness you have of your own mind. This chapter will present the advantages of meditation and heightened consciousness, as well as provide practical approaches on incorporating it into your daily life.

Exercise 9: Conscious Thoughts

Let's do a quick exercise. Set a timer for 2 minutes and try to clear your mind. During these 2 minutes, try to have no thoughts. You can do it in a quiet area or a loud one, with your eyes closed or open. Simply allow sensations to pass through you. Experience them, but refrain from passing judgment. Stop reading and do it right now.

Welcome back. Chances are, unless you're already proficient at this, you weren't able to think about absolutely nothing. But you were probably more aware of any thoughts you did have. You were more conscious of the presence of your thoughts, which is a far cry from the constant white noise of a chaotic thoughtstream.

What was the tone of your thoughts? Was it mostly positive or negative? When thoughts intruded your conscious periphery during the exercise, did you reprimand yourself or were you more accepting? There's a big difference between thinking "why can't I do this simple exercise? What's wrong with me" and "interesting. I wonder why it's difficult to clear my mind." These thoughts are a slice of life, a look into the often unobserved undercurrents of your mind. The more you set time aside to observe your thoughts, the better you'll be able to weed out negative patterns and direct your thoughts consciously.

Benefits of Meditation

Contrary to popular belief, meditation doesn't have to be time-consuming, nor does it have to be tied to any particular spiritual belief. Countless people have reaped the rewards of meditation, experiencing decreased anxiety, reduced stress, and improved sense of calm and optimism. One study shows that practicing meditation is at least as effective in reducing depressive symptoms as taking antidepressants, without any of the side effects.

The way it works is by strengthening the neural pathways from the frontal lobes of the brain, also known as the thinking brain. The thinking brain is what gives humans an edge over other animals, but it tends to disengage during stressful events, forcing us to default to our mammalian (limbic system) and reptilian (brainstem) brains. These parts of the brain often don't make decisions according to your higher interests. An example is when the fear of public-speaking triggers the fight-or-flight response, and your heart's leaping up to your dry throat, plus you have to pee really badly. Doesn't help you deliver a better speech.

Mindfulness is the state of consciously engaging all parts of the brain to become more aware of yourself and your surroundings, and meditation is the tool to get there. Frequent meditation practice enables you to re-engage the thinking brain even in stressful situations. Strategic mindfulness will help you master decisiveness in the following areas:

- **Perception:** by setting aside time to carefully observe your thoughts, you'll become more aware of what you really want.

- **Practice:** by frequently catching your thoughts in the midst of their formation and choosing to observe them or let them pass, you'll become better equipped to move onto the next step: choosing your own thoughts.
- **Presence:** by paying attention to the current moment, you'll be able to divorce it from the momentum of your past. You'll break free from considerations of sunk costs, as well as your decision-making patterns from the past.

"Know thyself."

- Socrates, legendary philosopher

To fix something, we must know how it works. Before I started meditating, I used to feel guilty out of the blue. These feelings didn't draw attention to themselves, but rather cast my life in a subtle shade of blue. I often felt bad as a person without knowing why. When I first started meditating, I often thought it was a waste of time because I had no realizations during the act. But then I realized my heightened awareness followed me long after the meditation sessions. Eventually, I saw the connection between my guilt and any time someone else had a negative feeling, even when it wasn't my "fault," like if a friend didn't like a movie I chose to see.

After solving the mystery, I devised the stupid simple solution of deciding not to feel bad for other people's feelings. My thinking brain knew that I wasn't responsible for other people's feelings, but my subconscious was slow to catch on. There's a refractory period for the subconscious to get with the times, but eventually it comes around. When you pull subconscious shadows into the light, you can override old patterns.

Picking the Approach

There are many different approaches to the art of meditation, and no one approach is better than the other. In the context of this book, **the primary purpose of meditation is practicing being more aware of any thoughts you have, in order to identify and change (if you want) preexisting thought patterns.** Thus, whichever method helps you most in that regard is gold. You can also use multiple approaches, as well as experiment until you find an approach that works for you.

One popular method involves trying to clear your mind and think about nothing. Some people prefer to set a timer while others rely on their internal clocks to determine when they should stop and ease out of the meditation. In any case, the goal is to reach a state of mindful presence, and become so accustomed to it that you spontaneously enter this state throughout the day even when you're not actively practicing meditation. In this state, you'll be able to make decisions with the full capacity of your conscious mind rather than unconsciously repeating ingrained patterns.

Another method is to incorporate a personal mantra into your meditation. Think of it as an opportunity to reconcile your stubborn subconscious with the beliefs you wish to have. My own mantra bounced around throughout the years, but eventually settled upon this: "I am here. The best time is now. The only time is now. Have no fear because the universe is abundant. I am a goddess manifesting my own destiny. I am not the receiver of reality; I am the creator of reality." This mantra helped me remember and solidify the beliefs that were true for me:

- **"I am here."**

  There will always be places I'd rather be and circumstances I'd rather have, but here is where I am. I can waste time moping about it, or recognize that here is what I have to work with.

- **"The best time is now."**

It might suck that I didn't start something important yesterday, but now is a great time too. The present is as good of a time as ever to do and be and feel anything I want. There's no need to wait for an arbitrary point in the future when I'll be ready or accomplished enough.

- **"The only time is now."**

I can't go back to the past to do something, nor can I skip to the future. I can only seize the present to do important, meaningful, fulfilling and pleasurable things. Now is what I have to work with when building good habits and creating positive emotions.

- **"Have no fear because the universe is abundant."**

The one thing keeping me from pursuing what I want is the fear of loss. One wrong decision and the good thing is gone. But I never had the good thing in the first place. There was a time when I didn't have my current job, my current boyfriend, my suitcase the airline carelessly lost, and I was just fine. My happiness isn't attached to external factors, but emerges from a universal energy within myself. External objects and circumstances come and go, but this abundant energy remains.

- **"I am a goddess manifesting my own destiny."**

I might have been dropped into a particular place with a particular set of circumstances, but now I have the awesome responsibility to create my future with my current choices and actions.

- **"I am not the receiver of reality; I am the creator of reality."**

My perceptions are not inevitable reactions to the external world, but rather conscious creations of my own experience. Most of the time, my creations are automatic, such as always feeling sad when someone calls me an idiot. Thus, it can *feel* like an inevitable reaction. But becoming aware of this process allows me to choose my own experiences and reactions.

Your meditation mantra is a great tool for shepherding your subconscious beliefs into alignment with your conscious, rational and strategically beneficial beliefs. We've all had the experience of knowing something logically but being unable to *believe* it on an emotional level. Practicing meditation helps bridge the gap.

Distill a concept or belief you'd like to have into a simple and powerful sentence that resonates with you, and work it into your mantra. For example, you could adopt the mantra "I am choosing my life right now" to remind you of the concepts in Chapter 1 of this book or "I respect my desires" to remind you of Chapter 8. Construct sentences that encapsulate entire beliefs and in time, they will penetrate the subconscious sphere.

"The thing about meditation is: you become more and more you."
- David Lynch, visionary filmmaker

Building the Habit

The first rule of habit building is to not be so dramatic about it. This may come as a shock in a world where people proclaim they'll run a marathon every morning and eat a low-carb high-fibre raw organic vegan diet the day after binge-drinking on New Year's Eve, but there's a reason New Year's resolutions fail. **To make any lasting change, we must consistently overcome subconscious resistance until it becomes the *new* subconscious pattern.**

The subconscious mind loves the familiar. For change to sneak its way past the gate, subtlety is key. The big change that inspires the conscious mind also scares the subconscious mind. And in a tug of war, the subconscious always wins. As the chief of regulating your heart rate and basal metabolic temperature, the subconscious simply works longer hours. To be successful in building a habit, choose goals that elicit neither inspiration nor a sense of challenge, say meditating for one minute each day. No pressure. Once the habit becomes second nature, you can gradually increase the duration.

To integrate a new habit, tie it to an existing habit, an activity you already perform daily, like brushing your teeth in the morning. After days of meditating immediately after brushing, your subconscious will start linking the two actions together to form one habit chain. Soon, the new action becomes an automatic response. If even one minute seems like a challenge to fit into your busy life, you can meditate *while* brushing your teeth. Instead of staring into the mirror and letting random thoughts wash over you, practice repeating your mantra or clearing your mind.

Exercise 10: Connecting a Change

Think of one change that has the power to transform your life, like exercising more or becoming more confident. Perhaps you've tried to make it into a habit, but it didn't stick. Revisit that habit and ask yourself what its bare minimum form is. For example, if your goal was to jog for half an hour every morning, the bare minimum would be to put on your jogging gear and step out the door.

Implementing the bare minimum version of an idealistic goal feels ridiculous at first, but you'll be surprised by how quickly you can build a habit when there's little psychological resistance. Since you've already overcome the hardest part - getting past the inertia of the previous activity and starting a new one, you'll tend to pass the mark (say running around the block), which is great, but never feel you have to surpass your original goal. Anything more than stepping out the front door counts as extra.

Tie your new action to an existing habit, whether it's getting in your car to go to work in the morning or having dinner. Once the relationship between the trigger activity and the reaction has been solidified, or when you no longer have to remind yourself of your new habit, you're ready to gradually work your way up from the bare minimum towards the most effective version of your habit.

Chapter 10
The Art of Intuition

Perhaps you've heard of the expression "your brain is smarter than you." So smart that you sometimes feel like you just know something without being able to explain why. Following our gut instinct, or spidey senses, has helped humans survive and evolve over millennia, but at this point in history, many see the gift of intuition as sentimental at best and superstitious at worst. This chapter will make a case for the gut, and reacquaint you to its ancient wisdom, so you can make decisions with greater speed and accuracy.

"Truly successful decision-making relies on a balance between deliberate and instinctive thinking."
- Malcolm Gladwell, journalist, author and speaker

The Science of Intuition

You've probably experienced a scenario that was something like this: you're at a dope party, but a nagging voice in your brain tells you to leave. You can't pinpoint why, but the feeling in the pit of your stomach is unsettling enough that you obey. Sure enough, you find out the next day that the police raided the house and a few kids got in trouble. Or perhaps you didn't heed your gut and had to face the consequences.

How did you know? Some would say it was coincidence, since no one can predict the future. Although researchers are looking into precognition, the phenomenon of anticipating events in the near future without the presence of sensory cues, like somehow knowing when someone will make eye contact with you, studies suggest that **intuition works not by seeing the future,**

but through the process of unconscious pattern recognition.
Your brain can perceive patterns before it can articulate said patterns through language and logical reasoning.

One study asked shogi (a Japanese board game akin to chess) players to make a checkmate move in less than one second. Far too little time for a game that usually lasts hours, yet many experienced players were able to pull it off. Brain scans of the individuals revealed that the frontal cortex, the area of the brain responsible for conscious thought, remained inactive. What lit up was the basal ganglia, the area responsible for habit formation and automatic behaviors. In contrast, there was little brain activity in the less experienced players, and they were unable to accomplish the checkmate move. One likely explanation is that the experienced players have seen the various board arrangements so many times that they're able to unconsciously grasp the pattern and react accordingly.

Just as some are experts at strategy games, we are the experts of our own lives. The more times we encounter situations in our field, whether it's filing legal reports or crossing the street, the more our subconscious accumulates patterns to help us act faster. Chances are you didn't predict the future that night at the party, but your subconscious recognized enough unsavory signs to trigger a response before your conscious mind could put a name to them. After all, when a car is coming right at you, you know you're in danger far before you're able to list the stimuli (increasing size of vehicle with no hint of deceleration) that tipped you off.

The Problem with Pros and Cons Charts

Your gut instinct isn't only good at keeping you alive. It also helps you make decisions that are traditionally analyzed with a sober mind and T-chart. One study reveals that people who buy a house based on their gut feeling are more likely to be satisfied with their choice than people who spend more time deliberating.

Pros and cons charts attempt to arrive at a neat integer by assigning a numerical value to each aspect of a decision. Noisy neighbors? -3. Nice balcony? +1. It sounds reasonable enough, until we remember how smart our brains are. If you give it space and time, your T-chart will fill up. You'll start to notice all sorts of things about the house you wouldn't have otherwise (nice door handles. +1. Blinds don't shut smoothly. -5).

But the thing is, the things you don't notice right away, the things you have to remind yourself to focus on, those are the things you'll *always* have to remind yourself to focus on. Those are the things that aren't important to you. They only made it onto the page because you were testing your brain's creativity. It's like two well-meaning friends having a conversation. One is trying to convince the other that it doesn't matter if the man's face makes her vagina shrivel up as long as they share the same interests, and the other is asking how she can enjoy activities with someone who doesn't excite her. They're both right, according to their own values.

When making a decision, like whether to move to another country for a job, if you need to actively remind yourself of the pro of experiencing a different culture, you'll likely need to remind yourself to enjoy this perk after making the decision. Likewise, if the con of being away from friends occurs to you far down the T-chart, it was probably of low priority to you in the first place. And if you choose to stay because of it, you might need to remind yourself of this con to avoid regret. Low priority factors that unfortunately influence decisions end up being justifications after the fact. **We make pros and cons charts to avoid bias, but the way we enjoy the outcome of a decision *is* biased.** Perhaps it's time to listen to your intuitive bias.

In one amusing experiment, researchers asked students to choose between posters of impressionist paintings and pictures of animals to take home. One group was asked to analyze their decision and write down the reasons for their choice while the other group was asked to choose without having to provide any justification. The study found that the latter group was happier with their decision, and was even more likely to display the newly acquired art in their homes. Researchers attribute this effect to verbal overshadowing, the process of putting into words what we've already understood intuitively. Apparently, some things can get lost in translation.

I suspect one possible explanation for the results of this experiment lies in our need to make things sound good for others and for ourselves. Engaging the language centers of the brain invites us to communicate our choices in a way that others would easily understand, and in doing so, we might pick the most impressive-sounding choice over the best choice.

In the book *When I Say No, I Feel Guilty*, Manuel J. Smith lists ten assertive rights to keep in mind to avoid being manipulated by others, among which are the right to to offer no justifications for your behaviors, the right to be illogical in making decisions, and the right to say "I don't know" when someone asks the whys of your choice. Manipulative people often consciously or unconsciously use seemingly apparent logic to undermine the soundness of our decisions, and we often internalize the voices of these manipulators such that they drown out the voice of our own intuition. We can avoid manipulating ourselves away from our best interests by reminding ourselves that logic is only one of many decision-making tools.

The Second Brain

From an evolutionary perspective, some of the most important choices humans had to make prior to modern food safety revolved around what to eat. Is it nutritious? Does it provide enough calories? Will it kill me? It makes sense that there's a direct line of communication between the digestive system and the brain. Billions of neurons carry signals from the brain to the gut, but also in the reverse direction. The microbes in your gut produce 50% of your dopamine and 90% of your serotonin (the feel-good hormones). Your gut rewards you for the right decisions, and not only when it comes to food.

Some researchers theorize that our gut bacteria promote pro-social behaviors in their hosts like group bonding to ensure the proliferation of their own species. The microbes look out for themselves by looking out for you. This is why gut health is a great indicator of emotional and mental health. In one experiment, researchers raised mice in a sterile lab where no bacteria could reach them. The mice started exhibiting signs similar to autism. Fortunately, the researchers were able to treat them with probiotics, and the little critters returned to normal.

In a similar vein, your gut bacteria signal their own dietary preferences, which you experience as cravings. For example, a diet high in sugar and other refined carbs encourages the proliferation of bacteria that survive on sugar. These bacteria then signal to the brain to consume more sugar, feeding the cycle.

The millions of microbes we share our lives with are intelligent. Their well-being can affect our own moods. After all, who hasn't experienced getting cranky and irritable after switching to a new diet or skipping a meal? No wonder the gut is sometimes referred to as the second brain. By listening to it, we can become more in tune with our intuitive knowledge and desires.

Tuning In

Ever tossed a coin to decide between two options? And when the coin landed, you suddenly knew what you wanted all along. Either you were relieved it landed on the option you wanted, or you were disappointed by the result (in which case you probably rationalized your way into defying the coin's sacred command). But why couldn't you hear your intuition sooner?

The indecisive mind prefers the illusion of open possibilities over the finality of a good decision. Even when one option is clearly better than the other, you can get stuck in the comfort of indecision. When the coin imposes its own finality, it forces you to see the finality you prefer. The next time you're at a crossroads, flip a coin and gauge your emotions. Are you more relieved or upset?

Exercise 11: Sensing Intuition

For the rest of the week, pick a relatively inconsequential area of life that you frequently encounter, yet have trouble making decisions in, like what to cook for dinner or what to wear to work. When making the decision, try to do it swiftly by identifying your gut instinct, and following it. Your gut instinct tends to be:

- **First:** The first option you think of tends to be your intuitive preference. Try to latch onto your first thought despite the turbulent stream thoughts that come after it.

- **Quiet:** Your intuition manifests as a deep inkling for a particular option, but it's not as loud as logic, which can shout its reasons and justifications. Your intuition is often unaccompanied by the seductive sway of words because it has traveled to you faster than your linguistic pathways.

- **Persistent:** Like still waters that run deep, your gut instinct exists on a separate plane from your logical faculties. While your conscious mind argues one point at a time, your subconscious pervades through all the arguments, such that you can still ruminate over one option long after the decision has been made.

Observe what your personal gut instinct sounds and feels like. Since you're practicing in areas of little to no consequence, you should be able to experiment fearlessly. Once you become familiar with the sensations of going with your gut, you'll naturally be able to graduate to bigger decisions, like decisions concerning career and family. In listening to your gut, you're relinquishing your own preconceived notions of what you want, and uncovering your true desires.

The Exceptions

Although following your gut is more likely to bring you satisfaction when it comes to big decisions, studies show that analysis is superior when it comes to smaller purchases, like home appliances and electronics. This makes sense because such products have quantifiable specs and features that aren't apparent upon first glance. For example, if you're buying a camera, the amount of megapixels and memory capacity might be more important than your first impression.

Another exception to the benefit of following your gut is when your gut is stuck in a negative pattern. Perhaps your conscious mind knows that there's nothing wrong with occasionally saying no to a friend, but you get a bad feeling every time you do. In such a case, it's not that your gut instinct is wrong, but that it's reacting to outdated patterns. Maybe in your childhood, your parents were abnormally harsh with you every time you said no, and now your subconscious senses danger in refusing others. If you notice negative emotional response patterns, it's better to gradually align your subconscious to the wisdom of your conscious mind.

Chapter 11
The Art of Momentum

A small, effortless change creates energetic momentum towards that direction, whether it's a positive change or a negative one. To master decisiveness at critical moments, the first step is to confidently make everyday decisions. This chapter will provide techniques to help you become more decisive in smaller situations, and to amplify them towards bigger situations.

The Domino Effect

Ever made a small improvement in one area of your life, like drinking more water, and had it spill into other areas of your life? Or maybe you couldn't resist having just one cookie, only to have your entire diet fall into disarray? Seemingly small decisions create their own momentous pattern. One decision leads to others like it. Welcome to the domino effect.

Perhaps you've had the experience of leaving your dirty dishes in the sink two nights in a row, only to have your entire kitchen turn into a mess a week later. On the flip side, if you make one corner of your apartment spotless, it'd be hard to resist cleaning the rest of the apartment. Likewise, the cleanliness of your apartment can spread to the rest of your life, and you might find yourself cleaning up your diet too. Your brain naturally seeks to avoid cognitive dissonance, so it'd take tremendous discipline to keep one side of the room neat and the other side messy. We like picking sides.

If you want to change your life, don't focus on total transformation. It's inspiring, but inspiration's not enough for successful action. On the contrary, a grandiose vision is detrimental, because the scope is too large. We wouldn't know where to start. To make matters worse, your subconscious resists because it seems like too much work. **To make progress, start small in the right direction. Then, the big transformation will take care of itself.**

But how can we trust that the new and improved decision pattern will prevail over old habits? If you clean one corner of a room, will the other three corners make it dirty, or will you be compelled to clean the other corners as well? Thanks to the sunk cost effect, the answer is almost always a clean room. Because you've already expended energy making one corner clean, it seems like a waste for it to get dirty again. The brain hates lost effort, so we continue to get the job done. It might seem like the larger negative patterns in your life would devour a small change, but the behavior you choose now has momentum on its side.

Exercise 12: Changing Your Environment

For this simple exercise, if your room is messy, clean one corner of it, or clean one surface, like the top of your desk or dresser. Don't be surprised if you can't stop. If your room is already clean, place an item that you love in a prominent position, and put into storage an item that you associate with negative emotions, or throw it away altogether. Affecting your immediate physical environment is one of the most powerful changes you can make because:

- Keeping your space clean and clutter-free soothes the subconscious, reducing stress and uplifting the mood.
- Your home is a physical representation of your inner self. Making it an authentic representation of who you are can lead to improved self-esteem and a greater sense of harmony.
- It demonstrates the power you have over your external environment. It reminds you that although the outside world often affects your feelings, the direction of influence also flows the other way.

If your living space is already arranged exactly the way you want it (lucky you,) make a one-time change that will have lasting benefits, like organizing the files on your computer, or switching to a slightly less annoying cable company. Again, don't be surprised if the improvements spread to other areas of your life.

Exercise 13: Practicing With Small Decisions

If you get comfortable with making small-scale decisions, your skill will naturally spread to bigger decisions. Pick any of the following exercises to practice making quick and confident decisions:

- Decrease the amount of time it takes for you to decide what to order at a restaurant you're unfamiliar with. Better yet, go to one of those custom food places, like custom burgers, and make some quick decisions.
- Decrease the amount of time it takes for you to decide what to wear to an important event.
- Pick something to watch on Netflix, fast.
- Purchase two tickets to an event when you have no idea who would want to go with you. Here, it pays to decide early because if you decide to ask your crush, they're less likely to be busy. And if they are busy, or aren't interested, you have plenty of time to ask someone else, or sell the extra ticket.
- Tell the party host you'll be bringing something special when you have no idea what you're bringing. The sooner you decide, the more time you'll have to prepare.
- Agree to show up to two simultaneous events. The sooner you choose one, the less offense it would cause when you cancel the other.

In a similar vein, be mindful of being decisive throughout the day no matter what the situation might be. Even if it's something you do every day anyway, like drinking a glass of water in the morning, try to think of it as you having decided to drink that glass of water.

Disrupting Patterns

Change is a glorious thing, but we're naturally resistant to it. After all, whatever we've been doing in the past has kept us alive up to now. Consider how strange it feels right after you rearrange your furniture. It might be more aesthetically pleasing and make more sense in your room, but the first couple of days will still feel refreshingly awkward. But after a week, it becomes the new normal. It might not feel like it, but you were choosing the previous arrangement every day. You just didn't perceive it, because it was a pattern. **Disrupting the invisible patterns in our lives trains our change receptivity, making us more aware of and willing to alter the bigger patterns as well.**

Exercise 14: Go the Other Way

On your morning commute to work or school, make it a point to alter your path just a little bit from what you're used to. Make your left turn at a slightly different point, or if you take public transit, get off a stop earlier. Observe your own discomfort surrounding such a change. Keep doing it day after day until the new path feels completely normal. Chances are, it's only going to take a few days. Pay close attention to your transition from feeling awkward about the new path to feeling like it's second nature.

It's a small change, but the dynamics are the same. Big changes and small changes alike consist of an awkward phase followed by a phase of ease, whether you're waking up five minutes earlier every day or building a whole new set of habits. The next time you're thinking of giving up on any positive change because it feels too hard, think back to this exercise. Remember that whatever changes you make will become easier and easier until it settles as a new pattern. By surviving day one of the change, you're already done with the hardest part.

Scaling Decisions

One of the hardest things about decision-making is committing to a long path when you aren't sure which path you want to be on. For a high school student to decide to be a computer programmer seems like a zero to a hundred decision. How can one take such a huge step? It becomes possible once you master the art of scaling decisions, the technique of starting with one low-commitment decision, then gradually implementing increasingly large decisions.

If your gut is telling you to be a programmer, but you can't make that decision, think about what programmers do. They write code. So instead of wallowing in wasteful indecision, simply decide, right now, to write a line of code. If you don't know how, decide to read a chapter on how to code. It's a low-commitment decision because one line of code isn't time-consuming. Plus, any action pierces through inertia and brings you one step closer to a certain decision. Do it again tomorrow, and the day after that. After a few days of these low-commitment decisions, it wouldn't be much of a jump to decide to write a line of code every day. You're already doing it. Soon, you can increase the lines of code written or chapters read per day.

Scaling decisions creates a slope that lifts you closer to certainty. If you're enjoying this process, you'll find it easier to achieve certainty and decide to become a programmer. If you've been miserable reading and coding, you'll decide you don't want to be a programmer. Either way, you achieve the mental stamp of finality. This technique can be applied to other areas of life. For example, if you can't decide whether you want a divorce, start by designating one hour of leisure time every day in which you're physically away from your spouse. Get out of the house if you have to. If you still miss them sometimes, that tells you something. If you feel a wave of incomparable relief, well, that tells you something else. Whichever decision you end up making, the technique of scaling decisions grants you more insight, and sometimes even new skills along the way.

Exercise 15: Ramp Up Your Certainty

Think of an unmade decision that has been bugging you lately. Make a list of everyday realities you would have to face in the event of choosing that path. For example, if the path in question is going back to school for your master's, part of the everyday reality would be going to classes, and depending on your circumstances, living more frugally. Pick one aspect and implement it immediately, whether it's committing to half an hour of independent study each day, or decreasing your entertainment budget. Gradually adopt more everyday realities until you can either commit to the path or back out with conviction.

Chapter 12
The Art of Immediacy

The thing that sets decisive and indecisive people apart is timing. We're all forced to act one way or another, but decisive people choose their course of action before they're forced. This is why decisive people seem to be pressing against the accelerator of life, breezing past stretch goals much faster than the average person. This chapter will help you make decisions at a more optimal time, and provide a method for sticking with your decisions.

Forcing Finality

Once you seal a letter, the contents are fixed. As soon as you hit "send" on an email, there's no retrieving it from the digital jungle. Decisive people take the initiative to apply their own stamp of finality while indecisive ones wait for their environment or other people to take the lead. Decisive people know which concert they want to go to before buying the ticket. An indecisive person might waver between two events until one event gets sold out. Decisive people have greater conscious control of their lives because they choose before their external environment chooses *for* them. To master decisiveness, practice imposing your own finality.

Consider this everyday scenario: you order steak at a restaurant. When was the point of finality? When you mentally decided what you wanted, or when you verbally told the waiter? What if after ordering the steak, you decide you want the salad instead? That definitely disrupts your finality. Do you achieve finality again when you inform the waiter of your new order? Do you achieve finality if the waiter tells you the chef has already started, so you can't change your order? But you can always order the salad in addition to the steak and pay extra. The point is,

externally applied finality is an illusion. Even if the restaurant only serves one dish, you can choose to leave.

The stamp of finality is a tool we use to save mental energy. Having a bunch of unmade decisions in the back of your mind is like leaving several programs running on the computer. You're not using any of them, but they still eat up your CPU. Because finality is self-imposed, you can lift it at any time. Maybe you've told everyone you know that you want to be an electrical engineer. You can still change your mind. Maybe you're already two years into your degree. The sunk cost creates a mental hurdle, but you can still change your mind. Counterintuitively, knowing you can change your mind allows you to commit more fearlessly to your decisions.

Overcoming Overload

When is the best time to make a decision? No set time is ideal. Since we have a finite amount of time, we want to make decisions as soon as possible. But we don't want to rush and end up being too rash. The key is to be able to **identify the point of diminishing returns, when additional information and feelings are no longer sufficiently relevant.**

As mentioned in Chapter 2, absolute certainty of outcome is impossible. We can never gather all the information on any particular topic. However, there is a point at which you've gathered most of the important, relevant information. Anything more would not only take a lot of time to dig up, but wouldn't be as pertinent to the decision at hand. Take the example of moving to another country. It's important to know the visa procedures, job market, standard of living and so on, and that might take several hours or days to research. However, it's possible to spend years researching every aspect of the country. At some point, it becomes clear that the different types of alpaca in Peru has little to do with your decision to live there.

Here, one can observe the 80/20 rule, which states that roughly 80% of the effects come from 20% of the causes. In this case, 80% of your enjoyment or unenjoyment of something comes from just 20% of the qualities of that thing. Thus, to avoid information overload, remember that it's not necessary to know everything about a situation in order to make an informed decision. Instead, focus on the 80%. First, determine what's most important to you. Is it sunny weather? Warm and friendly locals? Maybe it *is* the variety of alpacas. Once you have that figured out, you can seek out the corresponding info in a much more targeted and efficient manner.

The sister of information overload could well be emotional turbulence. Understandably, in addition to gathering reliable data, the brain also wants to feel sure before committing to a decision. The first inkling might be your trusty gut instinct, but for the decisions that require hard data, you'll find that in the time it takes to gather it, a bunch of different emotions would have clouded up your mental windshield. Feelings are fickle, approving one moment and disapproving the next. Remember that feelings are at least partially caused by hormones, and are a reaction to the external environment. To shift from passivity towards being active, it's crucial to make a decision after gathering enough relevant information despite that nagging feeling of uncertainty.

Decision Deadlines

As some of you know too well, it's hard to recognize the point of diminishing returns, especially towards the beginning of your journey towards greater decisiveness. Fear and paralysis keep us making excuses, rationalizing that it's never the right time to hunker down and choose. One fact that's hard to rationalize away is that time is finite, and unnecessarily stewing over a decision is a poor way to spend it.

As you gain more practice making decisions, you'll naturally start to determine the point of diminishing returns. But before that point, you can set your own deadlines for the troublesome decisions in your life, whether it's picking a career or picking where to go for dinner. **Ask yourself how much time you're willing to spend on the decision.** If it's two months, set your deadline two months from now. If it's one hour, set it one hour from now. And when the deadline arrives…

Write It Down

One tricky thing about decisions is sticking with them. Oftentimes, the mind remains unsettled after the exhausting mental acrobatics of making a decision, and continues to sift through the options like a broken record, imagining possible outcomes. Trusting one's own decisions requires confidence, which takes time to develop. The next best thing before reaching that point is taking action.

Exercise 16: Solidifying Decisions

Let's try this simple exercise for the rest of the day and tomorrow. Whenever you make a decision in your mind, no matter how small it is, (especially if it's small,) externalize the decision by writing it down. If there's no paper around, make a note on your phone or even text it to yourself. If you've been on the fence about going to that party tonight and you've just decided to go, write it down.

For the little decisions like washing the dishes or taking the trash out, you'll find that taking the time to write the note is almost more of a nuisance than the task itself. In such cases, do the task immediately after writing it down if it's possible to do so. You might feel like it's an interruption of whatever thing were doing before, but the thought of doing the task was already an interruption, and ignoring it only causes it to remain in your mind and weigh you down in subtle ways. If it's not possible to do the task immediately, writing it down is the next best outlet for the mind.

At the heart of it, decision-making takes place in the abstract realm of the mind. Having no tangible expression in the outside world, it's easy for us to go against our decisions, and even forget that we ever made them in the first place. This is why **it's crucial to externalize a decision as soon as possible after it's made. Writing down your decision is an easy way to take action in alignment with your decision, as well as provide a physical indicator of that decision.**

"A true decision is measured by the fact that you've taken a new action. If there's no action, you haven't truly decided."
- Tony Robbins, author of *Awaken the Giant Within*

Although writing down your decision is a powerful method, it's only a way to train yourself to take some form of action as soon as a decision is made. Once you get used to the pattern of immediately doing something after making a decision, you'll quickly find that there are other actions you can easily take in alignment with your decision. For example, after deciding to go to the party tonight, instead of writing it down, you can pick out what to wear and hang it in a prominent place. Both methods would succeed at quelling the thought of "oh maybe I shouldn't go after all" plaguing you late into the evening.

Your mind will actually hate the thought of having picked out that special outfit or written that note for no reason, which makes you more sure of your decision to go, and less likely to have second (third, fourth, fifth...) thoughts. In this sense, we can **use the sunk-cost illusion to our advantage by taking the biggest, boldest action after making a decision.** The most obvious example is me with airplane tickets. I could be so sure I want to go somewhere on such and such date, but thoughts of maybe not going will still pop up and make me stall on purchasing the ticket. The more I stall, the more ticket prices rise, making me even more unsure of whether or not I should go. So now I buy them and book accommodations as soon as I make the decision. And if I have to save up first, I do the next best thing of writing it down, and bookmarking the travel page for good measure.

Tough Decisions First

Imagine your mental agility as a fuel tank that gradually depletes throughout the day and recharges overnight. Researchers have found that willpower - the ability to choose what's best for you in the long term over more immediate pleasures - is a finite resource. Anyone who's excitedly started a strict diet in the morning only to binge on cupcakes come afternoon is all too familiar with this reality. We start off the day clear-headed, but the little inconsequential decisions (like what color of underwear to wear) we inevitably face throughout the day saps our mental energy. Decision-making is tough, and there is such a thing as decision-making fatigue. So to make the soundest decisions, do your heavy thinking earlier in the day.

Furthermore, the harder the decision, the heavier it weighs on the subconscious. It's best to get it out of the way as soon as possible, like ripping off a band-aid. And yet, the tough decisions are the ones we're most likely to avoid. For example, imagine Bob cheated on his partner and is trying to decide whether or not to tell her. He keeps putting off the decision, but the problem doesn't go away. It festers in the corner of his mind. **One way to avoid postponing difficult decisions indefinitely is by tackling them first thing in the morning.** It doesn't mean he has to tell her first thing in the morning, but he has to achieve the stamp of finality, and take the first action in alignment with his decision. Or at least give himself a decision deadline.

Chapter 13
The Art of Perspective

It can be nearly impossible to make a choice if you believe that choice will make or break your future. Your perspective radically influences your attitudes and behaviors in all aspects of life, including your decision-making style. It can sometimes feel like you're stuck with a certain perspective, but you can actually shift your perspective to better suit your needs. This chapter will provide a few visualization exercises to help you towards making bold and confident decisions.

Perceiving the Stakes

Imagine walking along a 1 foot wide beam raised slightly above the sidewalk. No big deal, right? Anyone could do it. But now imagine that the beam is raised high in the air, suspended between 2 skyscrapers. The beam is still 1 foot wide, but few people could walk along it at the same speed and with the same ease as they did on the lower beam. Many would be crippled by the height. For people struggling with making decisions, it feels like we're living life on the high beam.

The higher the beam, the higher the stakes of failure, and life seems to be the highest beam of all. But how serious is it really? Well, on the one hand, it's pretty serious, what with death, taxes, and other aspects of adulting. But then again, it's pretty silly, too. No matter what you do, no one comes out alive, and no one knows why. We're all just here for the ride. Your perspective determines whether you'll charge forward or cling to one spot in fear-induced paralysis.

The Fear Instinct

Our fears have a biological basis, and it's thanks in part to our ancestors' fear that we're here today. Failure way back in the day could mean starving to death or becoming a snack for the nearest carnivore. Some researchers even theorize that most humans tend to be risk-averse, as the more risk-taking individuals have had their population culled by natural selection. Their experiments reveal that generally, **people do not accurately gauge loss and gain. We're disproportionately averse to the risk of loss, even when it's outweighed by the potential gain,** which means missing out on favorable opportunities and investments.

For example, when participants were asked to choose between a Lindt Truffle for 26 cents and a Hershey's Kiss for 1 cent, most people aptly chose the truffle, as it was a good deal. However, when asked to choose between a truffle for 25 cents and the Hershey's for free, 90% of participants ended up choosing Hershey's, all to avoid the negative feelings caused by even the slightest of losses. This is why we have tools to calculate risks and benefits with impartiality.

We're lucky to be living in a time when our personal choices are rarely a matter of life and death, and failure often means an awkward moment, or simply starting over. But many of us aren't reaping the emotional benefits of a safer society. We aren't exercising the full extent of our freedom because somewhere in the back of our minds, we still fear risk and loss with the same intensity as our cavemen brethrens.

When you're afraid to wedge your way into that friend circle at a party, the response is physical. Adrenaline pumps through your veins, forming a lump in your throat and kicking your heartbeat into high gear, as if you were getting ready to run from a predator. It seems like a silly response, but let's remember that social rejection in a prehistoric context could mean being shunned by your hunter-gatherer tribe, which means no food, and you know the rest. It's nowhere near as dire now since we can just find another group to vibe with (through the power of the internet if we must). Our physiology just hasn't caught up to our improving circumstances yet.

The Bold Move

Some people are braver than others when it comes to taking risks, and they reap the benefits. They're more likely to seize opportunities that others are likely to pass up for fear of loss. More importantly, **the very quality of fearlessness can cause events to turn out in your favor,** simply because people tend to trust a bold and decisive leader.

Appearing fearlessly decisive almost gives you an air of godliness, because people will sense that for some reason, you aren't affected by the petty fears and doubts that plague everyone else. They will naturally gravitate towards you, even follow you under the subconscious assumption that maybe you know something they don't (which unfortunately explains the phenomenon of certain dictators and cults rising to power).

"Luck favors the bold. Leaders must fearlessly exploit the secret of decisiveness. Act boldly at critical moments."
- Toyotomi Hideyoshi, samurai and unifier of Japan

Robert Greene, the author of 48 Laws of Power discusses in length about the power of the bold move, which can only be accomplished by shifting your perspective. The bold move is so rare in our society that it can dazzle people and catch them off-guard. He even argues that part of the charm of children comes from the outlandish requests they make, and they make these requests devoid of the fear of rejection and failure. They're naturally confident and determined in getting what they want despite the circumstances. This is refreshing to most adults, who are hardened and disappointed by the years, and makes them envious of a time when they too wielded such boldness.

But how can one be unafraid when peering down from such a high beam?

Visualizing Detachment

Ever had a friend spill their guts to you about a "complex" problem, only to see the solution as black and white? It's so obvious to you what the best course of action is, but they can't see it. This is because they're in the midst of the problem, and their attachment to the possible outcomes induces fear and clouds their judgment. **To gain any degree of objectivity in our decision-making, we need a dose of detachment.** The following visualization exercises can pull you out from the thick of a heated problem:

Exercise 17: Setting the High Score

In the game of life, everyone's trying to get a high score. The point system will be different for different people. Perhaps to you, spending time with friends and family is worth more points than to Bob, who values rising in his career more. In a finite life, we all want more of what we value.

Imagine life as a fun video game that you only get to play once. In the world of games, the stakes are very high: rescue the princess or get eaten by a monster. But since it's a virtual reality, we perceive the stakes as very low, which allows us to navigate the game efficiently. No one would choose to stand still in one corner of the map, even though it would guarantee staying alive. Doing the opposite by intentionally flinging oneself off the nearest cliff also makes little sense. To get the highest score possible, you would simply play the game to the best of your ability, exploring the available world, experimenting with new skills, and making other reasonable choices to progress in the game.

In a video game, you don't waste time fighting the rules. You accept them and learn to use them to your advantage. Can all the creatures in the game fly except for you? So be it. No matter if you were born rich or poor, in the first world or a third world country, if your childhood was happy or sad, it's the only game you get. Rather than contemplate the fairness of the game's premises, accept your present reality as naturally as you accept that pressing the shift key will make your character jump. Only then can you move forward, and perhaps even begin to change some of the rules of society.

Exercise 18: Advice to a Good Friend

Chances are, when a friend comes to you with a problem or horrendous mistake, you take an empathetic approach. You want what's best for them, but there's no use being harsh and judging their past behaviors. Instead, you might warmly analyze their past mistakes for the purpose of learning from them, then try to devise a logical course of action for the future.

Many of us are too hard on ourselves. We're attached to our egos, which sometimes causes the best of us to do silly things, like fixate endlessly on a past blooper because we see it as a blemish on our idealized identities. What perfectionists often forget is that they're the only ones keeping such a close eye on their own score. Chances are, you wouldn't see your friend as less because of one mistake.

When you're imagining your own problem as a friend's problem, especially if you've been practicing the art of meditation, you'll start to separate your decision-making process from some of the more distracting feelings and sensations. For example, if your friend's health is jeopardized because they're overweight, you can be confident in your advice to them to lose weight, because you're not affected by the negative feelings associated with losing weight (like hunger pangs.)

Such feelings are deceptive because they often seem attached to an activity, like the thought of exercise triggering feelings of pain and laziness. In reality, feelings are fluid and often change as habit patterns change. We all know that exercise has mood-elevating properties. By maintaining a friendly distance towards your decision-making, you can avoid getting derailed by subconscious feeling associations.

Exercise 19: The Show Must Go On

A neat visualization exercise to try when you want to gain confidence and inner peace in unfamiliar situations is to imagine you're an actor playing a part in a theater, or on a film set. Assume that whatever comes out of your mouth are your lines, and you know your lines. The other person is just reading their lines. There's no way for the situation to go "wrong" because everything that happens is just the way the scene was written.

This concept can be applied to life on a grander scale. When going through a difficult situation, it's helpful to think of it as a scene in a film. No matter how dire it is, it will pass. You will inevitably move on to the next scene. Life, like a film, is composed of both good and bad scenes. The scenes of conflict, setbacks and disappointment are much more palatable when you remember that they're temporary.

You can also imagine you are the playwright, and the difficult choices you have to make in life are but unfinished portions of a script. You have an idea of how you want the play to end: with the accomplishment of your goals and dreams. The challenge is figuring out a plausible course of action with as few plot holes as possible. Viewing yourself as a character in a story gives you enough distance to analyze your actions and the consequences more realistically. For example, you would be more likely to see the relationship between hard work and success, rather than be trapped in an ego-driven delusion like good or bad things happen to a character because they "deserve" it.

A writer has the freedom to do some research if they find themselves writing about a topic about which they know little. But they're aware that they'll never really know if their scenes would unfold in the exact same way in real life. Still, they have a deadline to meet, and will commit to a storyline that makes enough sense. Likewise, you can never be sure if your future will work out exactly the way you intend, but at some point, you have to commit to a plausible course of action, lest be left with a blank page after running out of time.

The Freedom of Flow

The boldness and ease that often accompany detachment come more naturally when you truly don't care about the outcome. Life offers many examples of this. Men are generally better at talking to women they aren't attracted to. And many people have had the experience of acing an interview with a company they have little interest in, only to bomb the one they really care about. Ever see a kid play really well during practice, only to freeze up in the final game?

It seems cruelly ironic that performance quality often decreases when the stakes increase, but it makes perfect sense. **If a part of you is worried about the outcome, that's less attention**

distributed to the task at hand. In psychology, flow refers to the state of uninterrupted absorption in a challenging but fulfilling task. Think of a painter who forgets to eat and sleep as they're putting the final touches on their masterpiece. Understandably, it's hard to enter this state when the painter is worried about how much his work will sell for. No wonder self-help books like Mark Manson's *The Subtle Art of Not Giving a Fuck* have climbed up top-sellers lists.

Certain things are undoubtedly important in life, and that's not a bad thing. Caring deeply about certain matters gives you direction and purpose. We don't want to get rid of that, but there's a way to mimic the "give no fucks" attitude when approaching your goals: don't dwell on the outcome. Your mind is everything. As you might have noticed while practicing meditation and presence, how you choose to allocate your attentions drastically affects your emotional state and your behavior.

It sounds counterintuitive, what with all the conventional advice on visualizing your dreams coming true. **Once you've determined what it is you want and decided on a plan to get it, restrict thinking about the outcome to a few strategic milestones along the way,** just to check up on your progress. The less you think about your potential outcome, the less likely you are to get sucked into the spiral of self-doubt and second-guessing your chances of success, and the more time and attention you'll be able to devote to mastering the tasks along the way.

Section III Summary

1. Meditation can help you rewire your brain and gain greater control and perspective over your own thoughts and feelings. It's important not to get stuck in the dogma or stereotype of meditation and instead form an approach to mindfulness that caters to you. To make a habit of it, start with a tiny commitment until it sticks, then increase your goal over time.

2. Intuition is a legitimate form of intelligence, which works through the brain's subconscious recognition of patterns. Intuition can guide us towards our true desires when objectivity fails us. It takes conscious practice to tune in to the voice of intuition and decipher its message. Beware of gut responses created by false beliefs, such as while suffering from low self-esteem.

3. Little decisions will cause bigger changes than you think, since their momentum often sets off a chain of similar decisions. Disrupting one little pattern in our lives, like the route we take for our morning commute, can reveal a whole new layer of consciousness. Starting with an inconsequential decision in one direction then gradually scaling up as desired can bring you greater certainty - a much better strategy than waiting around hoping to magically feel sure about the decision.

4. Decisions aren't final until you say it is. It's better to apply your own mental stamp of finality before external circumstances apply it *to* you as options naturally diminish over time. Make a deadline for your decisions so you don't venture beyond the point of diminishing returns and waste your valuable mental energy. Writing down your decision is one of many ways to transform an abstract thought into tangible action. Because our willpower diminishes

throughout the day, it pays to make the tough decisions first.

5. People are overly risk-averse as a product of evolutionary strategy, but you can override this instinct through visualization. Practice viewing life through an analogous or detached lens to gain the benefits of acting boldly. Strive to reach the flow state as you're heading towards your goal, in which you take your eyes off the destination and become fully immersed in the tasks along the way.

Call to Action

Congratulations!

You're now equipped with all the theories and applications required on your journey towards mastering decisiveness. If you haven't been doing any of the exercises along the way, I relate. But now is time to spring into action.

It's almost addictive to sit around and absorb theories endlessly. It feels like we're accomplishing a great deal, but we aren't actually making a change in the day-to-day realities of our lives until we decide to take action. Even if it's 11:59 pm where you are, don't wait until tomorrow to take your first step.

The Myth of Tomorrow

"The future depends on what we do in the present."

- Mahatma Ghandi, pacifist leader

Tomorrow promises infinite possibilities. But does it deliver?

We often think we'll do all the difficult but necessary things tomorrow, and end up putting it off tomorrow as well. The potential of tomorrow is illusory, as the future is not yet real. In contrast, the opportunities of today are real and for the taking. If we consistently choose the hope of tomorrow over the potential of today, this decision in itself becomes a pattern that's very difficult to break.

The hope of tomorrow is a drug, filling you with the pleasure of inspiration and accomplishment, great emotional rewards for zero effort. In contrast, seizing the opportunities of today involves hard work. It's also the only way to see results.

Many people stuck in the trap of tomorrow mistakenly believe that they can wake up any day and choose today over tomorrow, completely ignorant of the "tomorrow pattern" they've been cementing this entire time.

You're constantly pivoting towards or away from your aim. There's no neutral path. So if you choose to diverge further from your goal today, you'll be even further tomorrow, and thanks to momentum, it will be even harder to get back on track. Fortunately, if you choose the right direction today, you'll be a little closer tomorrow, and the beneficial behavior will be a little easier to repeat.

Exercise 20: Seize the Day

Your final exercise combines the benefits of starting small and starting now. You can do it immediately even if you've been skipping all the previous exercises. Simply write on a piece of paper: I choose to be decisive today by _____.

Fill in the blank with one of the exercises, or even create your own exercise. Then, commit to applying the change at the very next opportunity. Refrain from overthinking and idealizing this first step. Remember that the purpose of this exercise is simply to create the first ripple of change that will spread to other areas of life and amplify over time.

"A year from now you will wish you had started today."

\- Karen Lamb, author

It matters little what you decide to do for the first step. Deciding to take the first step at all is an accomplishment in and of itself. With the completion of the previous exercise, you have commenced your journey towards a more conscious and decisive life.

About the Author

Calypso Guo writes about self-improvement, relationships, personality types and film. She also wrote several dating profiles before finally retiring. Her finished and unfinished screenplays sit in the attic. Just kidding, everything is digital nowadays. She dabbled in writing erotica under the top secret pen name Lilith James. Can't write resumes though.

She's the INFP half of INTJ & INFP Coffee, a youtube channel devoted to proving the validity of Myers-Briggs personality types, socionics and vultology. But really it's a place for an introvert to show off cute outfits which might otherwise never see the light of day.

Made in the USA
Las Vegas, NV
22 December 2023

83462844R00069